Texas GoMath!

Grade 2

Assessment Guide

- **Prerequisite Skills Inventory**
- **Beginning-of-Year, Middle-of-Year, and End-of-Year Benchmark Tests**
- **Module Tests in TEXAS Assessment Format**
- **Individual Record Forms**
- **Correlations to Texas Essential Knowledge and Skills for Mathematics**

Contents

Tests and Record Forms

Unit 4

Unit 5 (Module 19)

Unit 6 (Module 20)

Overview of *Texas GO Math!* Assessment

How Assessment Can Help Individualize Instruction

The *Assessment Guide* contains several types of assessment for use throughout the school year. The following pages will explain how these assessments can help teachers evaluate children's understanding of the Texas Essential Knowledge and Skills (TEKS). This *Assessment Guide* also contains Individual Record Forms (IRF) to help guide teachers' instructional choices to improve children's performance. The record forms may be used to monitor children's progress toward their mastery of the Texas Essential Knowledge and Skills for this grade.

Diagnostic Assessment

Prerequisite Skills Inventory in the *Assessment Guide* should be given at the beginning of the school year or when a new child arrives. This short answer test assesses children's understanding of prerequisite skills. Test results provide information about the review or intervention that children may need in order to be successful in learning the mathematics related to the TEKS for the grade level. The IRF for the Prerequisite Skills Inventory provides suggestions for intervention based on the child's performance.

Beginning-of-Year Test in the *Assessment Guide*, is multiple-choice format and should be given early in the year to determine which skills for the current grade children may already understand. This benchmark test will facilitate customization of instructional content to optimize the time spent teaching specific objectives. The IRF for the Beginning-of-Year Test provides suggestions for intervention based on the child's performance.

Show What You Know in the *Student Edition* is provided for each unit. It assesses prior knowledge from previous grades as well as content taught earlier in the current grade. Teachers can customize instructional content using the suggested intervention options. The assessment should be scheduled at the beginning of each unit to determine if children have the prerequisite skills for the unit.

Formative Assessment

Are You Ready? items appear in the *Assessment Guide*. These are quick checks to determine if children have the prerequisite skills they need for a particular lesson in the *Texas GO Math! Student Edition*. They may be reproduced for each child or shown to the class on a document camera. If several children have trouble with the Are You Ready? items, teachers may wish to review concepts before teaching the next lesson.

Middle-of-Year Test in the *Assessment Guide* assesses the same TEKS as the Beginning-of-Year Test, allowing children's progress to be tracked and providing opportunity for instructional adjustments, when required. The test contains multiple-choice items.

Summative Assessment

Module and Unit Assessments in the *Texas GO Math! Student Edition* indicate whether additional instruction or practice is necessary for children to master the concepts and skills taught in the module or unit. These tests include constructed-response and multiple-choice items.

Module and Unit Tests in the *Assessment Guide* evaluate children's mastery of concepts and skills taught in the module or unit. There is a test for each module. When only one module comprises a unit, the unit test assesses the content in just that module. When there are multiple modules in a unit, there are designated module tests and a comprehensive unit test. These tests contain multiple-choice items.

End-of-Year Test in the *Assessment Guide* assesses the same TEKS as the Beginning- and Middle-of-Year Tests. The test contains multiple-choice items. It is the final benchmark test for the grade level. When children's performance on the End-of-Year Test is compared to performance on Beginning- and Middle-of-Year Tests, teachers are able to document children's growth.

Using Correlations to TEKS

The final section of the *Assessment Guide* contains correlations to the TEKS. To identify which items in the *Assessment Guide* test a particular TEKS, locate that TEKS in the chart. The column to the right will list the test and specific items that assess the TEKS. Correlations to TEKS are also provided in the Individual Record Form for each test.

Assessment Technology

Online Assessment System offers flexibility to individualize assessment for each child. Teachers can assign entire tests from the *Assessment Guide* or build customized tests from a bank of items. For customized tests, specific TEKS can be selected to test.

Multiple-choice and fill-in-the-blank items are automatically scored by the Online Assessment System. This provides immediate feedback. Tests may also be printed and administered as paper-and-pencil tests.

The same intervention resources are available in the Online Assessment System as in the *Assessment Guide*. So, whether children take tests online or printed from the Online Assessment System, teachers have access to materials to help children succeed in *Texas GO Math!*

Data-Driven Decision Making

Texas GO Math! allows for quick and accurate data-driven decision making so teachers will have more instructional time to meet children's needs. There are several intervention and review resources available with *Texas GO Math!* Every lesson in the *Student Edition* has a corresponding lesson in the *Texas GO Math! Response to Intervention Tier 1 Lessons* online resource. There are also *Tier 2 Skills* and *Tier 3 Examples* available for children who need further instruction or practice. For online intervention lessons, children may complete lessons in *Soar to Success Math*. These resources provide the foundation for individual prescriptions for students who need extra support.

Using Individual Record Forms

The *Assessment Guide* includes Individual Record Forms (IRF) for all tests. On these forms, each test item is correlated to the TEKS it assesses. There are intervention resources correlated to each item as well. A common error explains why a child may have missed the item. These forms can be used to:

- Follow progress throughout the year.
- Identify strengths and weaknesses.
- Make assignments based on the intervention options provided.

1. Which number does this model show?

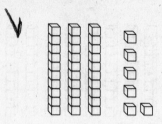

- ○ 35
- ○ 63
- ● 36

2. How many tens are there in the number 23?

- ○ 5 tens
- ● 2 tens
- ○ 3 tens

Name Tiwa

1. Which is the unknown number?

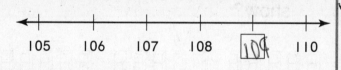

- ○ 119
- ● 109
- ○ 108

2. Which sentence is true?

- ○ 10 is greater than 100.
- ○ 18 is greater than 43.
- ● 50 is greater than 40.

Name Tiwa

1. Which number is the same as
1 ten?

- ○ 1
- ● 10
- ○ 100

2. Which number is the same as
10 tens?

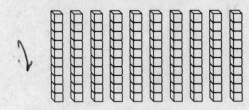

- ○ 1
- ○ 10
- ● 100

Name Tiwa

1. Which number does the model
show?

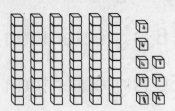

- ● 68
- ○ 65
- ○ 86

2. Which number does the model
show?

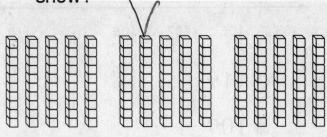

- ○ 100
- ● 150
- ○ 30

Name Tiwa

1. Which is another way to
write 57?

○ 70 + 5

○ 70 + 7

● 50 + 7

2. How many hundreds, tens,
and ones does the model
show?

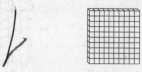

○ 1 hundred 4 tens 0 ones

● 1 hundred 0 tens 4 ones

○ 0 hundreds 1 ten 4 ones

Name Tiwa

1. Which is another way to write the number 30?

○ three

○ thirteen

● thirty

2. Which is another way to write the number 61?

○ sixteen   ● sixty-one   ○ sixty

1. Which shows the same number?

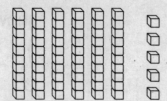

○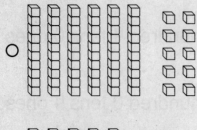

○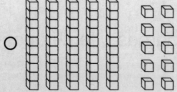

●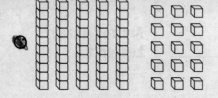

---

2. Which shows the same number?

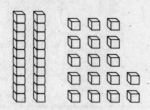

● 37

○ 27

○ 32

Name __Ti Wa__

1. Which number can be written as $400 + 50 + 8$?

   ● 458

   ○ 548

   ○ 485

2. Which is another way to write the number 832?

   ○ $80 + 30 + 2$

   ● $800 + 30 + 2$

   ○ $800 + 20 + 30$

Name __Ti Wa__

1. Which of these numbers is greater than 93?

   ○ 89

   ● 95

   ○ 91

2. Which of these numbers is less than 55?

   ● 49

   ○ 60

   ○ 57

1. Which is true?

   ○ 239 = 179

   ◉ 239 < 179

   ○ 239 > 179

2. Which is true?

   ○ 519 < 572

   ◉ 519 > 572

   ○ 519 = 572

1. Which of the following numbers would be a point between these two numbers on the number line?

   24   35

   ○ 38   ○ 23   ◉ 29

2. Which number is next in the skip counting pattern?

   80, 90, 100, 110, 120, 130, __140__

   ○ 120   ◉ 140   ○ 135

1. Which is the number?

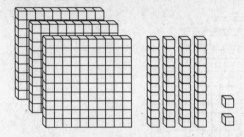

Hundreds	Tens	Ones
3	4	2

● 342

○ 353

○ 843

2. How many tens are there in one hundred?

○ I ten

◉ 10 tens

○ 5 tens

1. Which is the number?

two hundred ninety-one

○ 290   ● 291   ○ 201

2. Which is another way to write this number?

$$500 + 10 + 7$$

○ 607   ○ 570   ● 517

Name Ti Wa

1. Which number is the same as 10 hundreds?

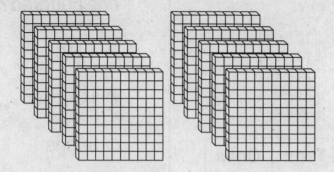

○ 100

○ 10

◉ 1,000

2. Which is the number?

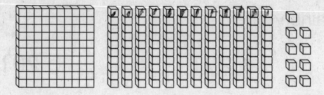

○ 1,129

○ 129

◉ 229

1. Which symbol makes the comparison true?

$$824 \bigcirc 789$$

- ○ >
- ● <
- ○ =

2. Which number is greatest?

- ○ 344
- ○ 276
- ● 351

---

1. Which comparison is true?

- ● 599 > 1,163
- ○ 1,145 > 1,055
- ○ 720 < 702

2. Which comparison is true?

- ● 1,200 < 1,174
- ○ 1,052 = 1,059
- ○ 999 < 1,000

Name _Tiwa_

1. Which shape shows equal parts?

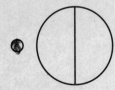   ○    ○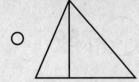

---

2. Which shape shows equal parts?

○ 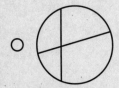   ○ 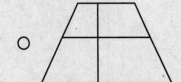   ●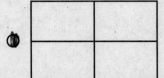

- -

Name _Tiwa_

1. What are the equal parts of this shape called?

○ fourths

● halves

○ eighths

2. What are the equal parts of this shape called?

● fourths

○ halves

○ eighths

1. How many fourths are in one whole?

  ○ 3

  ○ 2

  ◉ 4

2. How many eighths are in one whole?

  ◉ 8

  ○ 2

  ○ 4

✂ -

Name ___T iwa___

1. Which shape shows fourths?

 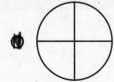   ○    ○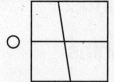

2. Which shape shows eighths?

○ 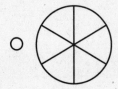   ◉    ○

Name ___Tiwa___

1. Which amount is shaded?

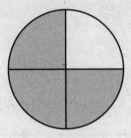

   ○ 2 fourths

   ○ 4 thirds

   ● 3 fourths

---

2. Which amount is shaded?

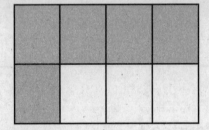

   ○ 5 fourths

   ● 5 eighths

   ○ 8 fifths

Name Tiwa

1. Which number sentence matches the cubes?

  ● 3 + 4 = 7

  ○ 7 + 2 = 9

  ○ 5 + 1 = 6

2. Which number sentence matches the cubes?

  ○ 8 + 2 = 10

  ● 6 + 2 = 8

  ○ 4 + 2 = 6

Name Tiwa

1. How many counters are needed to have 10 counters in all?

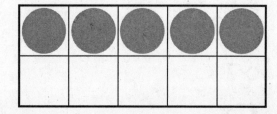

  ○ 4

  ● 5

  ○ 3

2. How many counters are needed to have 10 counters in all?

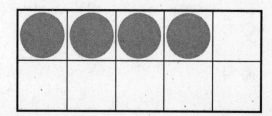

  ● 6

  ○ 4

  ○ 5

Name Tiwa

1. What is the missing addend?

$$6 + \boxed{2} = 8$$

- ○ 6
- ○ 1
- ● 2

2. What is the missing addend?

$$3 + \boxed{7} = 10$$

- ● 7
- ○ 8
- ○ 6

Name Tiwa

1. What is the difference?

$$10 - 6 = \boxed{4}$$

- ○ 5
- ● 4
- ○ 7

2. What is the difference?

$$10 - 2 = \boxed{8}$$

- ○ 12
- ○ 7
- ● 8

Name Tiwa

1. What is the sum?

$3 + 8 = 11$

○ 12

○ 10

● 11

2. What is the difference?

$12 - 5 = 7$

● 7

○ 8

○ 6

1. Which shows how you can make a ten to find the sum?

$8 + 6 =$ _____

○ $10 + 6 =$ _____

○ $10 + 4 =$ _____

○ $8 + 10 =$ _____

2. Which shows how you can make a ten to find the sum?

$7 + 9 =$ _____

○ $10 + 6 =$ _____

○ $7 + 10 =$ _____

○ $9 + 10 =$ _____

✂

1. $25 + 8 =$ ■

○ 38

○ 24

○ 33

2. $7 + 49 =$ ■

○ 47

○ 56

○ 54

1. What is another way to write 12?

   ○ 12 tens

   ○ 1 ten 2 ones

   ○ 1 ten 12 ones

2. What is another way to write 17?

   ○ 70 + 1

   ○ 1 + 7

   ○ 10 + 7

1. What is the sum?

   59 + 6

   ○ 55

   ○ 65

   ○ 61

2. What is the sum?

   53 + 4

   ○ 93

   ○ 67

   ○ 57

Name ĪĪWajope

1. Which is the sum?

$$\begin{array}{r} 11 \\ +\ 8 \\ \hline \end{array}$$

- ○ 19
- ○ 118
- ○ 29

2. Which is another way to write 87?

- ○ 8 tens
- ○ 8 tens 7 ones
- ○ 87 tens

Name _____

1. Which is the sum?

$$\begin{array}{r} 56 \\ +\ 33 \\ \hline \end{array}$$

- ○ 99
- ○ 23
- ○ 89

2. Which is the sum?

$$\begin{array}{r} 73 \\ +\ 24 \\ \hline \end{array}$$

- ○ 97
- ○ 57
- ○ 94

1. Which is the missing number in the related facts?

$$\boxed{9} + 8 = 17$$
$$17 - \cancel{8} = 8$$

- ○ 2
- ○ 9
- ○ 7

2. Which is the missing number in the related facts?

$$6 + \blacksquare = 18$$
$$18 - 6 = \blacksquare$$

- ○ 12
- ○ 18
- ○ 14

Name _____

Are You Ready?
Lesson 7.4

1. Which is the sum?

$$\begin{array}{r} 8 \\ 5 \\ + 2 \\ \hline \end{array}$$

- ○ 10
- ○ 15
- ○ 13

2. Which is the sum?

$$\begin{array}{r} 7 \\ 6 \\ + 3 \\ \hline \end{array}$$

- ○ 13
- ○ 20
- ○ 16

1. Which is the sum?

$$\begin{array}{r} 26 \\ 37 \\ + 13 \\ \hline \end{array}$$

○ 76

○ 39

○ 63

2. Which is the sum?

$$\begin{array}{r} 34 \\ 19 \\ + 63 \\ \hline \end{array}$$

○ 107

○ 97

○ 116

Name _____

1. Which completes the tens fact?

$$10 - \underline{\quad} = 8$$

○ 7

○ 2

○ 8

2. Which shows a way to break apart 7?

○ $7 - 2 = 5$

○ $7 + 2 = 9$

○ $10 - 7 = 3$

Name _____

1. Which is the same as 18?

○ $10 + 8$

○ $80 + 1$

○ $1 + 8$

2. What is 10 less than 26?

○ 36

○ 62

○ 16

1. Which is the difference?

$$11 - 3 = \underline{\hphantom{00}}$$

- ○ 8
- ○ 9
- ○ 7

2. Which is the difference?

$$15 - 9 = \underline{\hphantom{00}}$$

- ○ 7
- ○ 9
- ○ 6

1. Which addition fact does the model show?

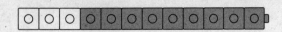

- ○ $3 + 9 = 12$
- ○ $6 + 6 = 12$
- ○ $3 + 7 = 10$

2. Which is the difference?

$$34 - 18$$

- ○ 52
- ○ 16
- ○ 24

1. Subtract 35 from 62. How many tens and ones are in the difference?

Tens	Ones

○ 2 tens 7 ones

○ 2 tens 3 ones

○ 3 tens 7 ones

2. Subtract 23 from 76. How many tens and ones are in the difference?

Tens	Ones

○ 4 tens 9 ones

○ 4 tens 3 ones

○ 5 tens 3 ones

1. Which is the difference?

Tens	Ones
7	8
− 4	5

○ 33

○ 23

○ 32

2. Which is the difference?

Tens	Ones
8	2
− 6	7

○ 25

○ 15

○ 35

1. Which is the difference?

$$68 - 17$$

- ○ 49
- ○ 51
- ○ 41

2. Which is the difference?

$$70 - 48$$

- ○ 32
- ○ 38
- ○ 22

1. Amanda has 37 beads. Carla has 29 beads. Which number sentence can be used to find how many beads they have?

- ○ $37 - 29 = \blacksquare$
- ○ $37 + 29 = \blacksquare$
- ○ $37 + 9 = \blacksquare$

2. Joe read 26 pages and Max read 40 pages. Which number sentence can be used to find how many more pages Max read than Joe?

- ○ $26 + 40 = \blacksquare$
- ○ $26 - 4 = \blacksquare$
- ○ $40 - 26 = \blacksquare$

1. Which is the difference?

$$\begin{array}{r} 93 \\ -\ 72 \\ \hline \end{array}$$

○ 21

○ 11

○ 25

2. Which is the difference?

$$\begin{array}{r} 75 \\ -\ 31 \\ \hline \end{array}$$

○ 44

○ 34

○ 36

1. Find the sum.

$$82 + 45 = \blacksquare$$

○ 138

○ 117

○ 127

○ 37

2. Find the sum.

$$29 + 93 = \blacksquare$$

○ 122

○ 64

○ 111

○ 112

1. Find the sum.

$$38 + 29 = \blacksquare$$

○ 51

○ 67

○ 9

○ 57

2. Find the sum.

$$19 + 45 = \blacksquare$$

○ 55

○ 54

○ 26

○ 64

1. Find the sum.

$$90 + 30 = \blacksquare$$

- ○ 60
- ○ 130
- ○ 120

2. Find the sum.

$$60 + 80 = \blacksquare$$

- ○ 140
- ○ 120
- ○ 20

1. Find the sum.

$$310 + 450 = \blacksquare$$

- ○ 770
- ○ 760
- ○ 140

2. Find the sum.

$$155 + 245 = \blacksquare$$

- ○ 390
- ○ 400
- ○ 90

Name _____

1. Find the difference.

   $27 - 19 = $ ▓

   ○ 8

   ○ 46

   ○ 36

2. Find the difference.

   $60 - 35 = $ ▓

   ○ 95

   ○ 25

   ○ 35

✂

Name _____

1. Find the difference.

   $240 - 112 = $ ▓

   ○ 352

   ○ 138

   ○ 128

2. Find the difference.

   $340 - 115 = $ ▓

   ○ 235

   ○ 225

   ○ 455

1. Find the difference.

$$921 - 834 = \blacksquare$$

- ○ 87
- ○ 755
- ○ 97

2. Find the difference.

$$655 - 249 = \blacksquare$$

- ○ 417
- ○ 416
- ○ 406

1. Solve.

$$350 - \blacksquare = 111$$

- ○ 249
- ○ 261
- ○ 239

2. Solve.

$$254 + \blacksquare = 682$$

- ○ 428
- ○ 438
- ○ 936

1. What is the value of a nickel?

- ○ 5¢
- ○ 10¢
- ○ 1¢

2. What is the total value?

- ○ 5¢
- ○ 50¢
- ○ 32¢

1. What is the value of a quarter?

- ○ 10¢
- ○ 5¢
- ○ 25¢

2. What is the total value?

- ○ 75¢
- ○ 15¢
- ○ 55¢

1. Which is the total value?

○ 31¢

○ 36¢

○ 21¢

2. Which is the total value?

○ 75¢

○ 41¢

○ 71¢

1. Which coin has a value of 10 cents?

○ dime

○ nickel

○ quarter

2. Which is the value of a quarter?

○ 5¢

○ 25¢

○ 10¢

Name _____

1. Find the sum.

$$8 + 9 + 4 + 3 = \blacksquare$$

○ 21

○ 24

○ 17

2. Find the sum.

$$6 + 6 + 6 + 6 + 6 = \blacksquare$$

○ 24

○ 36

○ 30

Name _____

1. Find the sum.

$$9 + 9 + 9 + 9 = \blacksquare$$

○ 36

○ 27

○ 45

2. Find the sum.

$$8 + 8 + 8 + 8 = \blacksquare$$

○ 24

○ 32

○ 40

1. There are 4 equal groups of counters. Each group has 3 counters. How many counters are in the groups?

   ○ 15

   ○ 12

   ○ 16

2. There are 7 equal groups of counters. Each group has 2 counters. How many counters are in the groups?

   ○ 21

   ○ 9

   ○ 14

1. Ellen has 3 boxes of buttons. There are 6 buttons in each box. How many buttons does Ellen have?

   ○ 18

   ○ 15

   ○ 24

2. Jake has 5 bags of marbles. There are 4 marbles in each bag. How many marbles does Jake have?

   ○ 15

   ○ 20

   ○ 9

1. There are 27 counters. There are 3 equal groups of counters. How many counters are in each group?

   ○ 24

   ○ 30

   ○ 9

2. There are 30 counters. They are in equal groups of 10 counters. How many groups are there?

   ○ 40

   ○ 20

   ○ 3

1. Heather has 12 birds and 4 cages. She puts an equal number of birds in each cage. How many birds are in each cage?

   ○ 3

   ○ 16

   ○ 8

2. Colin has 18 tomato plants. He plants them in equal rows of 9 plants. How many rows of tomato plants are there?

   ○ 27

   ○ 2

   ○ 9

1. How many groups of
   2 counters can be made
   with 8 counters?

   ○ 6

   ○ 3

   ○ 4

2. How many groups of
   2 counters can be made
   with 12 counters?

   ○ 6

   ○ 10

   ○ 5

1. Which is another way to write
   5 hundreds 4 tens 7 ones?

   ○ 547

   ○ 754

   ○ 475

2. Which is another way to write
   8 hundreds 3 tens 0 ones?

   ○ 83

   ○ 830

   ○ 803

1. Which is 10 more than
   1,084?

   ○ 1,074

   ○ 1,048

   ○ 1,094

2. Which is 10 less than 763?

   ○ 762

   ○ 753

   ○ 773

---

1. Which is the sum?

   36 + 24 = ▪

   ○ 60

   ○ 52

   ○ 62

2. Which is the missing addend?

   27 + ▪ = 46

   ○ 21

   ○ 73

   ○ 19

1. Which is the difference?

$$85 - 51 = \blacksquare$$

○ 26

○ 34

○ 24

---

2. Which is the missing number?

$$72 - \blacksquare = 45$$

○ 33

○ 27

○ 37

1. Which is a name for this shape?

○ square

○ triangle

○ circle

2. Which shape has 4 sides?

○

○

○

1. How many vertices does a hexagon have?

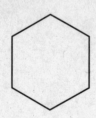

○ 4

○ 6

○ 5

2. Which is a name for this shape?

○ quadrilateral

○ square

○ pentagon

1. How many sides does this shape have?

○ 4 sides

○ 8 sides

○ 6 sides

2. How many vertices does this shape have?

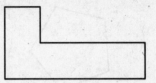

○ 6 vertices

○ 2 vertices

○ 5 vertices

✂ -

1. Which shape has more than 5 sides?

○

○

○

2. Which shape has fewer than 6 vertices?

○

○

○

Name _____

1. How many sides does this shape have?

○ 6 sides

○ 4 sides

○ 5 sides

2. Which two blocks can be put together to make this shape?

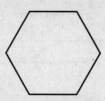

○ ▱ and ▱

○ ▽ and △

○ △ and ▱

Name _____

1. Which is a shape that has only 4 vertices?

○ hexagon

○ quadrilateral

○ triangle

2. Which is a shape that has fewer than 5 sides?

○ octagon

○ pentagon

○ triangle

Name _____

1. Which of these solids is a
triangular prism?

○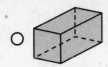

○

○

2. Which of these solids is
a cone?

○

○

○

- -

Name _____

1. How many vertices does a
cube have?

○ 12

○ 8

○ 9

2. How many edges does a
triangular prism have?

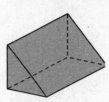

○ 6

○ 12

○ 9

1. Colton built a rectangular prism using unit
cubes. How many unit cubes did Colton use?

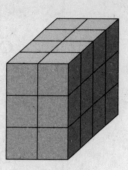

   ○ 24

   ○ 26

   ○ 12

---

2. Amber builds the first layer of a rectangular
prism using 15 cubes. She adds another layer.
How many cubes are used for the prism?

   ○ 25

   ○ 17

   ○ 30

Name _____

1. About how long is the crayon?

○ about 1 ■ long

○ about 4 ■ long

○ about 3 ■ long

2. About how long is the pencil?

○ about 5 ⬭ long

○ about 3 ⬭ long

○ about 4 ⬭ long

- -

Name _____

1. A color tile is about 1 inch long. About how many inches long is this string?

○ about 4 inches

○ about 1 inch

○ about 5 inches

2. A color tile is about 1 inch long. About how long is the string?

○ about 2 inches

○ about 4 inches

○ about 1 inch

Name _____

1. Use an inch ruler. Which is the length of the pencil to the nearest inch?

○ 4 inches

○ 5 inches

○ 2 inches

---

2. Use an inch ruler. Which is the length of the paper clip to the nearest inch?

○ 1 inch

○ 4 inches

○ 2 inches

1. Which line is longer than the string?

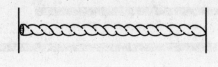

○

○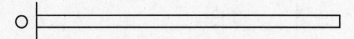

○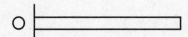

---

2. Which line is shorter than the pencil?

○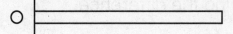

○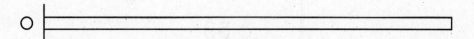

○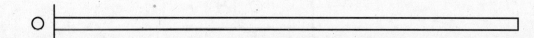

Name _____

1. About how long is the paintbrush?

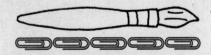

○ about 5 ◎

○ about 6 ◎

○ about 10 ◎

2. Which string is the longest?

A ▬▬▬▬▬▬▬▬▬

B ▬▬▬▬▬▬▬▬▬▬▬

C ▬▬▬▬▬▬▬▬

○ A

○ B

○ C

Name _____

1. Find the sum.

$$25 + 18 = \blacksquare$$

○ 45

○ 33

○ 43

2. Find the difference.

$$35 - 19 = \blacksquare$$

○ 53

○ 14

○ 16

1. Measure the length to the nearest centimeter.

    ○ 10 centimeters

    ○ 12 centimeters

    ○ 7 centimeters

2. Measure the length to the nearest centimeter.

    ○ 18 centimeters

    ○ 10 centimeters

    ○ 12 centimeters

---

1. Find the sum.

$$10 + 10 + 10 = \blacksquare$$

    ○ 30

    ○ 25

    ○ 20

2. Find the sum.

$$6 + 6 + 6 + 6 = \blacksquare$$

    ○ 18

    ○ 30

    ○ 24

1. Look at the clock. What time does it show?

○ 9:30

○ 8:30

○ 7:00

2. Look at the clock. What time does it show?

○ 12:00

○ 4:00

○ 4:30

1. Look at the clock. What time does it show?

○ 9:30

○ 7:00

○ 6:45

2. Look at the clock. What time does it show?

○ 12:15

○ 3:00

○ 12:00

I. Look at the clock. What time does it show?

○ 1:30

○ 1:25

○ 5:05

2. Look at the clock. What time does it show?

○ 8:00

○ 2:40

○ 8:10

I. Look at the clock. What time does it show?

○ 3:30

○ 7:15

○ 7:18

2. Look at the clock. What time does it show?

○ 11:22

○ 4:55

○ 11:30

Seeds Planted	
Vegetable	Tally
Carrot	ЖЖ
Broccoli	ЖЖ IIII
Corn	IIII

1. Use the tally chart.
How many carrot seeds were planted?

○ 5

○ 4

○ 9

2. Use the tally chart.
Which seed did most children choose to plant?

○ carrot

○ corn

○ broccoli

Books Checked Out					
Mystery	●	●	●		
Sports	●	●	●	●	●
Science	●	●			

Key: Each ● stands for 1 book.

1. Use the pictograph.
How many sports books were checked out?

○ 5

○ 2

○ 3

2. Use the pictograph.
Which type of book was checked out 3 times?

○ Sports

○ Science

○ Mystery

Types of Oranges					
Navel	●	●	●	●	
Pineapple Sweet Orange	●				
Temple	●	●			
Valencia	●	●	●	●	

Key: Each ● stands for 1 orange.

1. Use the pictograph. Which type of orange did most children choose?

○ Navel

○ Valencia

○ Temple

2. Use the pictograph. Which type of orange did the fewest children choose?

○ Navel

○ Pineapple Sweet Orange

○ Temple

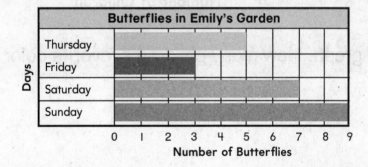

Butterflies in Emily's Garden

Days: Thursday, Friday, Saturday, Sunday

Number of Butterflies: 0 1 2 3 4 5 6 7 8 9

1. Use the bar graph. How many butterflies did Emily see on Saturday?

○ 5

○ 9

○ 7

2. Use the bar graph. How many more butterflies did Emily see on Sunday than on Thursday?

○ 5

○ 4

○ 9

Name _____

Bugs in the Backyard					
beetles	●	●	●		
ants	●	●	●	●	●
caterpillars	●	●			

Key: Each ● stands for 1 bug.

1. Use the pictograph. How many caterpillars were in the backyard?

○ 1   ○ 5   ○ 2

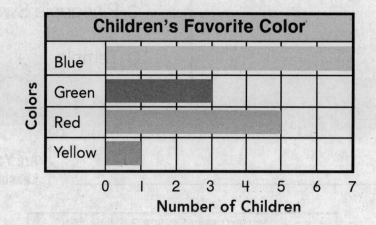

2. Use the bar graph. How many children's favorite color is Red?

○ 3   ○ 1   ○ 5

Toy Model Cars					
Blue Car	●	●	●		
Red Car	●	●	●	●	●
White Car	●	●	●		

Key: Each ● stands for 1 Toy Model Car.

1. Use the pictograph. How many toy model cars are either blue or red?

   ○ 8　　　　　　　○ 3　　　　　　　○ 5

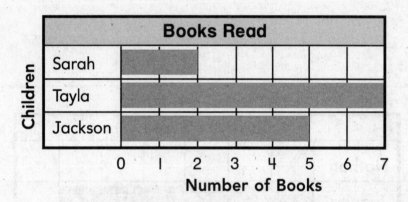

2. Use the bar graph. Which student read the most books?

   ○ Sarah　　　　　○ Tayla　　　　　○ Jackson

Colors of Flowers					
Red	●	●	●	●	●
Yellow	●	●			
Pink	●	●	●	●	

Key: Each ● stands for 1 Flower.

1. Use the pictograph. What color flower did Jonathon find the most of?

   ○ Red

   ○ Yellow

   ○ Pink

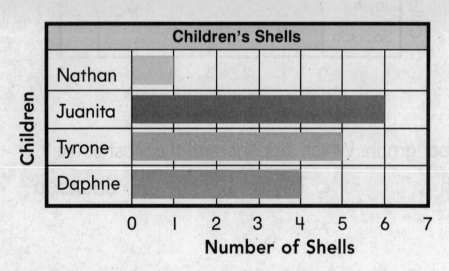

2. Use the bar graph. Which two students found a total of 10 shells?

   ○ Tyrone and Daphne

   ○ Nathan and Juanita

   ○ Juanita and Daphne

I. What is the total value of this group of coins?

○ 40¢

○ 4¢

○ 20¢

2. What is the total value of this group of coins?

○ 30¢

○ 60¢

○ 25¢

I. What is the next number in this skip counting pattern?

2, 4, 6, _____

○ 8

○ 5

○ 10

2. What is the next number in this skip counting pattern?

5, 10, 15, 20, _____

○ 30

○ 25

○ 26

1. What is the difference?

$$32 - 5 = \underline{\quad}$$

○ 28

○ 37

○ 27

2. What is the difference?

$$40 - 7 = \underline{\quad}$$

○ 34

○ 33

○ 47

1. What is the difference?

$$55 - 23 = \underline{\quad}$$

○ 32

○ 22

○ 72

2. What is the difference?

$$100 - 40 = \underline{\quad}$$

○ 96

○ 50

○ 60

1. Alice has 6 buttons. How many groups of 3 buttons can she make?

   ○ 4

   ○ 2

   ○ 3

2. Manny has 8 markers. How many groups of 2 markers can he make?

   ○ 6

   ○ 4

   ○ 10

1. There are 42 crayons in a bag. 24 crayons are taken out of the bag. Then 8 crayons are put into the bag. How many crayons are in the bag now?

   ○ 58

   ○ 26

   ○ 38

2. There are 53 crayons in a bag. 19 crayons are taken out of the bag. Then 23 crayons are put into the bag. How many crayons are in the bag now?

   ○ 67

   ○ 57

   ○ 95

Fill in the bubble for the correct answer.

1. Dean has 137 stickers.

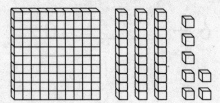

What is 137 in expanded form?

_____ + _____ + _____

2. Maria writes the number 87. What is a number that is less than Maria's number?

_____

_____

3. Use the number line to order the numbers.

<───────────────────────>

[ ] 96   97   [ ]   [ ]

What are the numbers in order from least to greatest?

_____ , _____ , _____

4. Write <, >, or =.

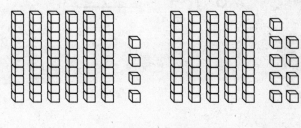

64 ◯ 59

GO ON ▶

5. There are 5 acorns and 2 squirrels. How many more acorns are there?

_____ more

6. Show a way to make 10. What number completes the addition sentence?

$$6 + \underline{\hspace{2cm}} = 10$$

7. There are 8 black sheep and 4 white sheep in the meadow. How many sheep are there?

$$8 + 4 = \underline{\hspace{2cm}}$$

8. How many pennies do you need to have the same value as a nickel?

1 nickel = _____ pennies

GO ON ➡

Name _____

9. Count. Write the total value.

_____ ¢   _____ ¢   _____ ¢   _____ ¢   _____ ¢   _____ ¢

---

10. Skip count. Write how many.

_____ shoes

11. Look at the chart. What is the unknown number?

10 Less	Number
	104

---

12. Luz has 5 big cups. She has 7 small cups. What is a number sentence that shows how many cups Luz has?

5	7

?

_____ + _____ = _____

GO ON

13. Jordan sees 15 birds in a tree. Some birds fly away. There are 8 birds still in the tree. What is a number sentence that shows how many birds fly away?

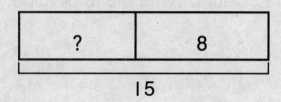

?	8

15

_____ − _____ = _____

---

14. What number makes expressions of equal value?

$11 - 2 =$ _____ $+ 2$

15. Write the unknown numbers.

$9 +$ _____ $= 17$

$17 - 9 =$ _____

---

16. What number completes the related fact?

$9 + 9 = 18$ and _____ $- 9 = 9$

17. Will describes a three-dimensional solid as big and green. Can you use these clues to name the solid? Write **yes** or **no**.

_____

GO ON

18. Look at the hexagon.

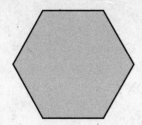

Write how many.

_____ sides

_____ vertices

19. Look at the cube.

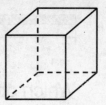

Write how many.

_____ faces

_____ edges

_____ vertices

20. Write numbers to complete.

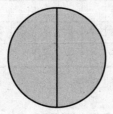

The circle is cut into _____ equal parts.

The picture shows _____ halves.

21. Look at the rectangle.

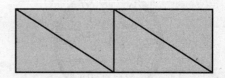

Does it show fourths?
Write **yes** or **no**.

_____

GO ON ➡

Name ______________________________

22. A box is the same length as this string.

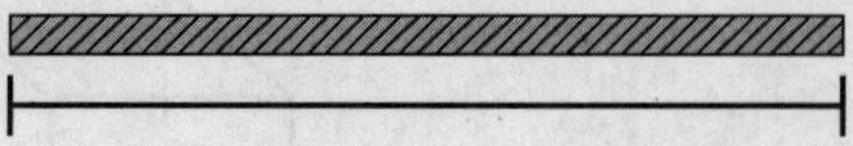

Which object will **NOT** fit in the box?

Write its name. ____________________

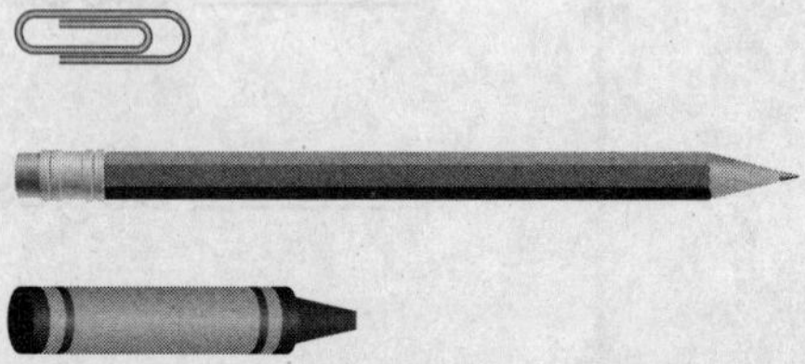

paper clip

pencil

crayon

23. Look at the hour hand. Write the time.

12
1
2
3
4
5
6
7
8
9
10
11

half past ______

24. Use the graph.

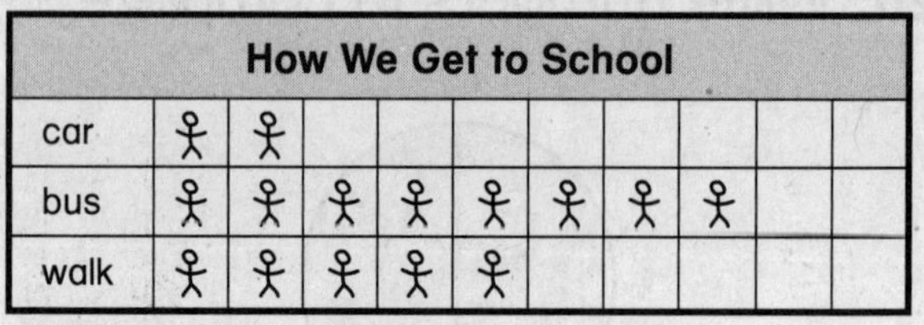
How We Get to School
car
bus
walk

Each 🯅 stands for 1 child.

How many more children take the bus than walk?

______ more children

25. Annie saves 10¢ each week for 5 weeks. How much money does Annie save?

______

STOP

Name _____

Fill in the bubble for the correct answer.

1. Which is another way to write two hundred sixty-five?

○ 256   ○ 265   ○ 562

2. Which could be the unknown number?

$$894 < \underline{\hspace{1cm}} < 1{,}172$$

○ 1,052   ○ 1,189   ○ 894

3. Owen drew this point on a number line.
Which could be Owen's number?

250   350

○ 300 + 20 + 5

○ 200 + 50 + 8

○ 500 + 80 + 2

4. Compare 458 and 588. Which of these is true?

○ 588 is greater than 458.

○ 458 is equal to 588.

○ 588 is less than 458.

5. Kirit draws a point on the number line. Which number belongs at the point?

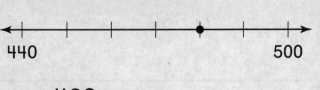

- ○ 490
- ○ 480
- ○ 470

6. Nate drew this shape. Which word describes the parts?

- ○ fourth
- ○ eighths
- ○ halves

7. Which word makes this sentence true?

Rectangle B has _____ equal parts than Rectangle A.

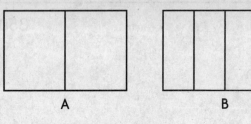

- ○ larger
- ○ smaller
- ○ fewer

8. Mona drew this shape.

What amount of her shape is shaded?

- ○ I fourth
- ○ 4 eighths
- ○ 4 fourths

GO ON ➡

9. Which shape shows equal parts?

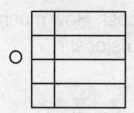

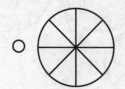

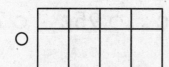

10. On Friday, there were 9 children at the park. On Saturday, there was double that number. How many children were at the park on Saturday?

○ 9

○ 17

○ 18

11. Diana makes bracelets at a craft store. On Thursday she makes 12 bracelets. On Friday she makes 9 bracelets. How many bracelets does Diana make on the two days?

○ 11   ○ 22   ○ 21

12. Dennis collects toy cars. He has 26 red cars. He has 7 more blue cars than red cars. How many toy cars does Dennis have?

○ 59   ○ 33   ○ 13

GO ON ➡

13. Jason and his sister blow up balloons for a party. They blow up 26 balloons in the morning and 37 balloons in the afternoon. How many balloons did they blow up?

○ 62

○ 63

○ 53

14. Ally is at a baseball game. She buys a bag of peanuts. These coins show what the peanuts cost. How much do the peanuts cost?

○ 90¢   ○ 95¢   ○ 70¢

15. Lana gives Graciela these coins. What is the total value of the coins?

○ 18¢   ○ 57¢   ○ 43¢

16. Ari has 3 bags. He has 8 juice boxes in each bag. How many juice boxes does he have?

○ 24   ○ 11   ○ 5

GO ON ➤

17. Sue has a bag of 12 apples . She shares the apples equally with 5 friends and keeps a share. How many apples does each person get?

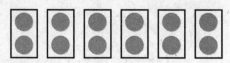

  ○ 17

  ○ 7

  ○ 2

18. There are an even number of boys and an odd number of girls in the school play. Which could be the number of boys and the number of girls?

  ○ 13 boys and 8 girls

  ○ 12 boys and 9 girls

  ○ 12 boys and 8 girls

19. Mick has 10 more stickers than Gillian. Gillian has 38 stickers. The number of stickers Fritz has is 10 less than the number Mick has. How many stickers does Fritz have?

   ○ 68   ○ 38   ○ 48

20. Terry has 35 stars on a chart. Mary put 16 more stars on the chart. What number sentence can be used to find the number of stars on the chart?

   ○ $35 - 16 = $ ■

   ○ $35 + 16 = $ ■

   ○ $16 + $ ■ $ = 41$

GO ON

21. Anna draws this shape. How many vertices does her shape have?

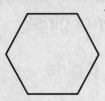

○ 8 vertices

○ 7 vertices

○ 6 vertices

22. Which of these solids is a cylinder?

○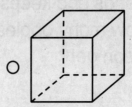

○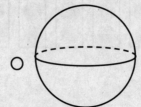

○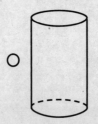

23. How many sides does this polygon have?

○ 10 sides   ○ 9 sides   ○ 8 sides

24. Ben put blocks together to make this shape. How many sides does his new shape have?

○ 10 sides   ○ 8 sides   ○ 6 sides

25. Mark folds this shape along the dashed lines. What new shapes did he make?

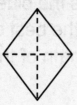

- ○ triangles
- ○ parallelograms
- ○ quadrilaterals

26. Tom measures the length of a box. He says the box measures 1 foot. Which is the same length as 1 foot?

- ○ 12 inches
- ○ 12 feet
- ○ 1 inch

27. Large chains are 15 inches long. Small chains are 4 inches long. Which shows how many are needed to have 38 inches of chain?

- ○ 1 large chain and 3 small chains
- ○ 2 large chains and 2 small chains
- ○ 1 large chain and 2 small chains

28. Janet has a piece of ribbon that she measures in centimeters. She draws this diagram to show its length. How long is her ribbon?

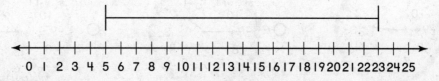

- ○ 17 centimeters
- ○ 18 centimeters
- ○ 28 centimeters

GO ON ➡

29. Billie chooses an object that is about 3 inches long. Which object did Billie choose?

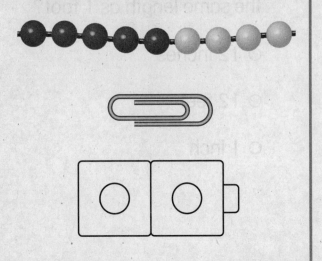

○ cubes ○ clip ○ beads

30. Pattie has a blue dresser that is about 4 feet long. She has a white dresser that is about half as long as the blue dresser. Which is the best estimate for the length of the white dresser?

○ about 2 feet

○ about 2 inches

○ about 20 inches

31. Ashley uses color tiles to make a rectangle. She uses 6 rows of tiles and 4 columns of tiles. How many tiles does Ashley use?

○ 10   ○ 24   ○ 64

32. Tad's softball game starts at 2:45. Which clock shows this time?

○    ○    ○

GO ON ➡

33. Jeff makes a pictograph to record the number of animals at the petting zoo. There are 12 goats at the petting zoo. How many ◯ will Jeff draw to show 12 goats?

Animals at the Petting Zoo						
Goats						
Rabbits						
Horses						

Key: Each ◯ stands for 2 animals.

   ◯ 12   ◯ 2   ◯ 6

34. Which question could you use the bar graph to answer?

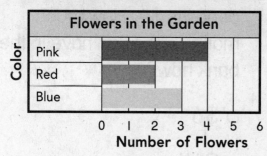

○ How many blue and purple flowers are there?

○ How many red and pink flowers are there?

○ How many people pick flowers?

35. Which describes the change shown in the data?

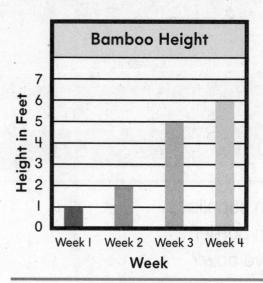

○ The height of the bamboo decreases from the first week to the fourth week.

○ The height of the bamboo stays the same from the first week to the fourth week.

○ The height of the bamboo increases from the first week to the fourth week.

36. Fred earns 8 dollars a week. Each week he spends 3 dollars and saves the rest. How long will it take him to save 30 dollars?

○ 8 weeks

○ 6 weeks

○ 5 weeks

GO ON ➤

37. Lon has $12 in the bank. He withdraws $6. Later he deposits $9. How much money does Lon have in the bank now?

    ○ $6

    ○ $14

    ○ $15

38. Jan wants to buy a pen that costs 98¢. She has 69¢ right now. How much money would she need to borrow to pay for the pen?

    ○ 29¢

    ○ 39¢

    ○ 38¢

39. Ava lends $16 to Suen Win. Suen Win pays the same amount to Ava each week and pays her all of the money in 4 weeks. How much did Suen Win pay Ava each week?

    ○ $16

    ○ $3

    ○ $4

40. Miss Smith has $25. She spends $15 on supplies to make a dish garden. She sells the dish garden for $30. How much money does she have now?

    ○ $30

    ○ $40

    ○ $55

Fill in the bubble for the correct answer.

1. Which is another way to write two hundred ninety-six?

   ○ 269   ○ 296   ○ 692

---

2. Which number makes the comparison true?

   _____ > 1,158

   ○ 1,172   ○ 1,118   ○ 825

---

3. Compare 547 and 677. Which of these is true?

   ○ 677 is greater than 547.

   ○ 547 is equal to 677.

   ○ 677 is less than 547.

---

4. Dennis drew this point on a number line.
   Which could be Dennis's number?

   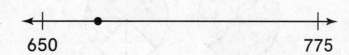

   650   775

   ○ 600 + 70 + 5

   ○ 600 + 50 + 7

   ○ 500 + 60 + 7

GO ON ➡

Name _____

5. Katy draws a point on the number line. Which number belongs at the point?

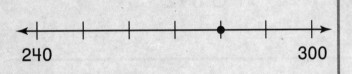

240   300

○ 290

○ 280

○ 270

6. Nick drew this shape. Which word describes the parts?

○ fourth

○ eighths

○ halves

---

7. Lela has 3 pieces of cloth that are the same size. She cuts the red cloth into 2 equal parts, the blue cloth into 5 equal parts, and the green cloth into 10 equal parts. Which cloth has the largest parts?

○ red cloth   ○ blue cloth   ○ green cloth

---

8. Which amount of the two shapes is shaded?

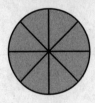 

○ 1 eighth

○ 4 eighths

○ one and 4 eighths

GO ON

25. Mae folds this shape along the dashed lines. Which new shapes did she make?

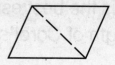

○ triangles

○ squares

○ parallelograms

26. Tara measures the length of a poster. She says the poster measures 1 foot. Which is the same length as 1 foot?

○ 12 inches

○ 12 feet

○ 1 inch

27. Eric uses a ruler to measure a book. It is 6 inches long. Which sentence is true?

○ 6 inches is the same as 6 feet.

○ 6 feet is a greater length than 6 inches.

○ 6 inches is a greater length than 6 feet.

28. Jameer has a piece of string that he measures in centimeters. He draws this diagram to show its length. How long is his string?

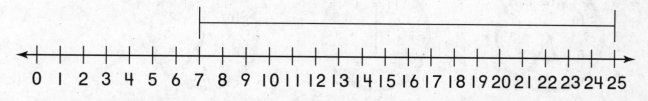

○ 16 centimeters   ○ 18 centimeters   ○ 32 centimeters

GO ON

29. Sadie chooses an object that is about 1 inch long. Which object did Sadie choose?

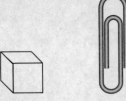

○ cube

○ coin

○ paperclip

30. Each side of a desk is 2 feet long. Carol's ribbon is about as long as 4 sides of the desk. Which is the best estimate for the length of Carol's ribbon?

○ about 8 feet

○ about 8 inches

○ about 16 inches

31. Alecia has 12 color tiles. She wants to make a rectangle with 4 rows and 4 columns. How many more color tiles does Alecia need?

○ 8   ○ 4   ○ 16

32. The hour hand points between the 5 and the 6. In 35 minutes it will be the next hour. Which clock shows what time it is?

○ A   ○ B   ○ C

GO ON →

33. Eric is making a bar graph to show the kinds of sandwiches his cousins like.

- 4 like cheese.
- 5 like tuna.
- 1 likes peanut butter.
- 2 like ham.

For which sandwich will he draw a bar that ends at the line for 4?

○ tuna   ○ ham   ○ cheese

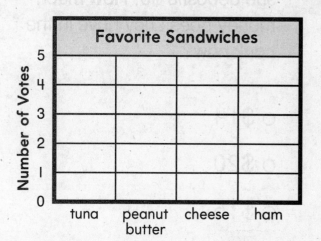

34. Use the pictograph. Which question could you use the pictograph to answer?

○ How many children voted for blue and orange?

○ How many more children voted for green than for blue?

○ How many children did not vote?

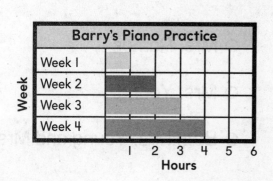

35. Use the bar graph. Which is the best prediction of how many hours Barry might practice piano in Week 5?

○ 6 hours

○ 1 hour

○ 6 minutes

36. Jamie saves 9 dollars each month. How much will she save in 5 months?

○ 14 dollars   ○ 45 dollars   ○ 36 dollars

GO ON

37. Lucy has $14 in the bank. She withdraws $5. Later she deposits $6. How much money does Lucy have in the bank now?

- ○ $14
- ○ $20
- ○ $15

38. Jude wants to buy a pad of paper that costs 75¢. He has 49¢. How much money does he need to borrow to buy the pad of paper?

- ○ 26¢
- ○ 36¢
- ○ 37¢

39. Casey lends $15 to Jackie. Jackie can give Casey $5 a week to pay her back. How long will it take for Jackie to pay Casey back?

- ○ 5 weeks   ○ 4 weeks   ○ 3 weeks

40. Mrs. Young makes a pair of curtains. She sells the curtains to Mrs. Ramos for $45. Who is the consumer?

- ○ Mrs. Ramos
- ○ Mrs. Young
- ○ Both Mrs. Young and Mrs. Ramos

Name _____

Fill in the bubble for the correct answer.

1. Kelly has 465 stamps. Which is another way to show 465?

   ○ $400 + 50 + 6$ ○ $400 + 60 + 5$ ○ $500 + 40 + 6$

---

2. There are 650 white pebbles in the garden. There are fewer black pebbles than white pebbles. How many black pebbles could there be?

   ○ 550   ○ 752   ○ 875

---

3. Which number makes the comparison true?

   _____ $> 1,057$

   ○ 1,168

   ○ 1,049

   ○ 957

---

4. Barbara drew this point on a number line to show the number of books she read.

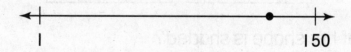

   Which could be Barbara's number?

   ○ $500 + 20 + 1$ ○ $200 + 50 + 1$ ○ $100 + 20 + 5$

GO ON

5. Kim draws a point on the number line. Which number belongs at the point?

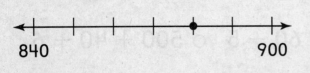

- ○ 890
- ○ 880
- ○ 870

6. Nan drew this shape. Which word describes the parts?

- ○ fourths
- ○ halves
- ○ eighths

7. Lexie has 3 loaves of bread that are the same size. She cuts the banana bread into 2 equal parts, the pumpkin bread into 4 equal parts, and the wheat bread into 12 equal parts. Which bread has the largest parts?

- ○ banana bread   ○ pumpkin bread   ○ wheat bread

8. Kelee drew this shape.

Which part of her shape is shaded?

- ○ I eighth   ○ 4 eighths   ○ one and 8 eighths

9. Which shape shows equal parts?

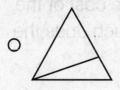

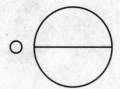

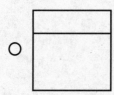

10. Which addition fact can you use to find $12 - 6$?

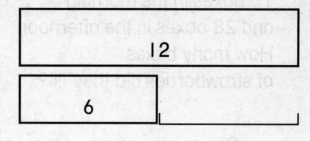

$$12 - 6 = \blacksquare$$

○ $6 + 4 = \blacksquare$

○ $6 + 6 = \blacksquare$

○ $6 + 12 = \blacksquare$

11. Shane had 36 marbles. He bought 24 more marbles. Then Billie gave him 12 marbles. How many marbles does Shane have now?

○ 72   ○ 60   ○ 50

12. Madison made 21 cheese pretzels. She made 12 plain pretzels. She gave 8 pretzels to her cousins. How many pretzels does she have now?

○ 35

○ 25

○ 15

13. Taissa and her brother pick strawberries. They fill 15 boxes in the morning and 28 boxes in the afternoon. How many boxes of strawberries did they fill?

○ 13

○ 33

○ 43

14. Amy is at the roller skating park. She buys a drink. These coins show the cost of the drink. How much does the drink cost?

○ 40¢

○ 45¢

○ 50¢

15. Bev has 52¢. Which is another way to write the amount of money that Bev has?

○ ¢0.52   ○ 0.52¢   ○ $0.52

16. Breta has 3 baskets. She puts 5 oranges in each basket. How many oranges does she use?

○ 15 oranges   ○ 12 oranges   ○ 8 oranges

GO ON

17. Eli has 16 baked potatoes. He places the same number of potatoes on each of 2 plates. How many potatoes are on each plate?

○ 8

○ 18

○ 14

18. There are an even number of ducks and an odd number of frogs at the lake. Which could be the number of ducks and the number of frogs?

○ 7 ducks and 3 frogs

○ 8 ducks and 3 frogs

○ 6 ducks and 2 frogs

19. Mr. Johns builds a wall with 255 bricks. Then 100 bricks fall to the ground. How many bricks are left in the wall?

○ 245   ○ 155   ○ 154

20. Juanita had 42 stamps on a card. Then she got 13 more stamps on the card. What number sentence can be used to find the number of stamps on her card?

○ $42 - 13 = \blacksquare$

○ $42 + 13 = \blacksquare$

○ $13 + \blacksquare = 42$

GO ON ➤

21. Paul draws this shape. How many vertices does his shape have?

○ 6 vertices

○ 4 vertices

○ 5 vertices

22. Which solid has five faces?

○ triangular prism

○ cube

○ rectangular prism

23. Which shape matches the sorting rule?

Shapes with more than 4 sides

○ 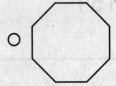   ○ 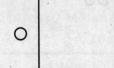   ○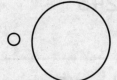

24. Carlos built this rectangular prism using unit cubes. How many unit cubes did Carlos use?

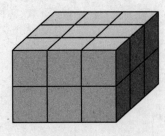

○ 16   ○ 17   ○ 18

GO ON

Name _____

25. Brooke folds this shape along the dashed line. Which new shapes did she make?

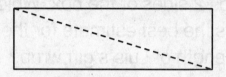

○ triangles

○ squares

○ rectangles

26. Toby measures the length of a scarf. She says the scarf measures 1 foot. Which is the same length as 1 foot?

○ 12 inches

○ 12 feet

○ 2 inches

27. Elana uses a ruler to measure a toy bench. It is 12 inches long. Which sentence is true?

○ 12 inches is the same as 12 feet.

○ 12 feet is a greater length than 12 inches.

○ 12 inches is a greater length than 12 feet.

28. Cassie's puppy has a collar that she measures in centimeters. She draws this diagram to show its length. How long is the collar?

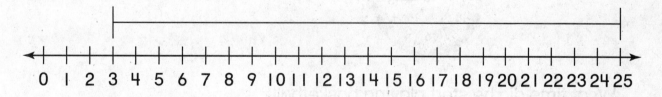

○ 23 centimeters   ○ 22 centimeters   ○ 27 centimeters

GO ON

29. Max chooses an object that is about 1 inch long. Which object did Max choose?

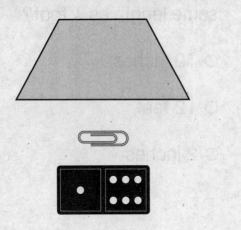

○ block   ○ clip   ○ domino

30. The sides of a box are 2 feet long. Luis has some gift wrap. The gift wrap is about as long as 2 sides of the box. Which is the best estimate for the length of Luis's gift wrap?

○ about 4 feet

○ about 4 inches

○ about 8 inches

31. Al has 15 color tiles. He wants to make a rectangle with 6 rows and 3 columns. How many more color tiles does Al need?

○ 9   ○ 3   ○ 18

32. David starts playing basketball at the time shown on the clock.

What time did he start playing basketball?

○ 1:02 P.M.   ○ 12:15 P.M.   ○ 1:45 A.M.

GO ON

33. Sam is making a bar graph about the juice his friends like best.

- 8 vote for grape juice.

- 2 vote for orange juice.

- 6 vote for apple juice.

For which juice will he draw a bar that ends at the line for 8?

○ apple   ○ orange   ○ grape

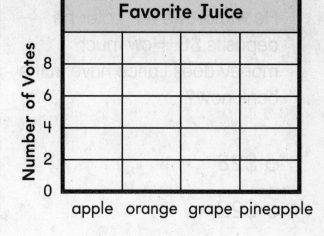

Use the bar graph for 34–35.

34. How many games did Claude play?

○ 4   ○ 8   ○ 6

35. Which question could you use the bar graph to answer?

○ How many children did not play?

○ Why did Kat play 2 games?

○ How many games did Ned play?

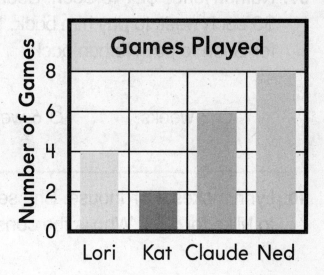

36. Janine saves 7 dollars each month. How much will she save in 6 months?

○ 13 dollars   ○ 42 dollars   ○ 35 dollars

GO ON

37. Lance has $16 in the bank. He withdraws $4. Later he deposits $8. How much money does Lance have in the bank now?

○ $28

○ $22

○ $20

38. Molly wants to buy a toy that costs 95¢. She has 58¢ right now. How much money would she need to borrow to pay for the toy?

○ 37¢

○ 43¢

○ 44¢

39. Nathan lends $21 to Sean. Sean can give Nathan $3 each week to pay him back. How long will it take for Sean to pay Nathan back?

○ 3 weeks   ○ 6 weeks   ○ 7 weeks

40. Lynn makes a birdhouse. She sells the birdhouse to Mike for $18. Who is the consumer?

○ Mike

○ Lynn

○ both Mike and Lynn

Fill in the bubble for the correct answer.

1. Which is another way to write four hundred thirty-seven?

   ○ 473

   ○ 374

   ○ 437

2. Together, Alfonso and his friend have 492 pennies. Which is another way to write 492?

   ○ two hundred ninety-two

   ○ four hundred ninety-two

   ○ nine hundred forty-two

3. Keisha has 328 buttons. What is another way to show 328?

   ○ 300 + 20 + 8

   ○ 300 + 80 + 2

   ○ 200 + 30 + 8

GO ON

4. Lindsi draws a point on the number line. What number belongs at the point?

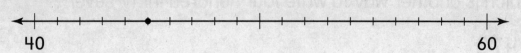

40   60

○ 47

○ 45

○ 50

5. There are 10 fish in each bowl. There are 12 bowls in all. How many fish are there?

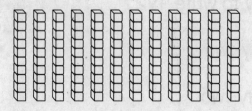

○ 201   ○ 112   ○ 120

6. Abeela uses blocks to show a number. She uses 7 ones blocks, 5 tens blocks, and 9 hundreds blocks. What number does she show?

○ 579

○ 957

○ 759

GO ON

7. My number has 4 ones, no tens, and I hundred.
Which is my number?

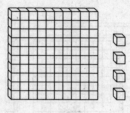

○ 104   ○ 140   ○ 401

---

8. Dawna has 124 pennies. Which is a way to show 124?

○ 100 + 20 + 4

○ 100 + 40 + 2

○ 400 + 20 + 1

---

9. What number belongs at the point on the number line?

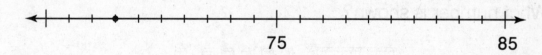

75   85

○ 65

○ 68

○ 74

GO ON

10. What number is shown?

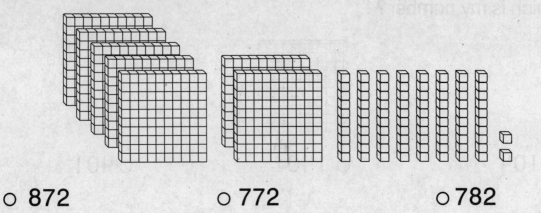

○ 872   ○ 772   ○ 782

---

11. Elliot draws this number line. What number belongs at the point?

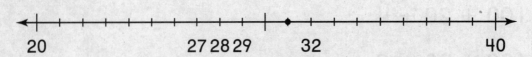

○ 35

○ 30

○ 31

---

12. What number is shown?

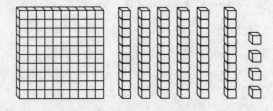

○ 164   ○ 146   ○ 416

STOP

Fill in the bubble for the correct answer.

1. What number does this quick picture show?

○ 4 hundreds 3 tens 5 ones

○ 400 + 30 + 6

○ four hundred twenty-six

2. Which quick picture shows 200 + 70 + 2?

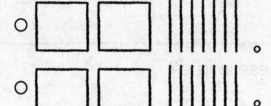

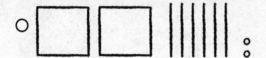

3. Which is another way to write 740?

○ 700 + 4

○ 70 + 4

○ seven hundreds 4 tens

GO ON

4. Which number has 8 tens?

○ 982

○ 800

○ eight hundred nine

---

5. Compare 636 and 366. Which of these is true?

○ 636 is greater than 366

○ 636 is equal to 366

○ 636 is less than 366

---

6. Compare 493 and 549. Which of these is true?

○ 549 < 493

○ 549 = 493

○ 549 > 493

GO ON

7. Jack has 173 ones blocks. Devon has 237 and Liz has 256 ones blocks. Which comparison is correct?

○ 173 < 237 < 256

○ 237 > 173 > 256

○ 256 > 237 < 173

8. At three movies, there are 182 people, 313 people, and 287 people. Which of these shows the numbers ordered from least to greatest?

○ 287 > 313 > 182

○ 182 < 287 < 313

○ 313 > 287 < 182

9. Olan drew this point on the number line to mark game points. Which could be Olan's number?

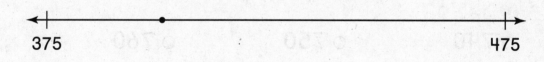

375   475

○ 500   ○ 445   ○ 400

GO ON

10. Jorge's favorite number is 500. Which point on the number line shows where 500 belongs?

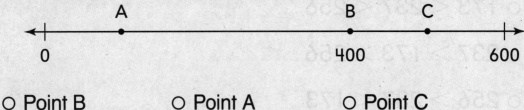

○ Point B   ○ Point A   ○ Point C

---

11. Mishaal draws a point on the number line. Which number belongs at the point?

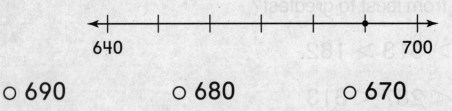

○ 690   ○ 680   ○ 670

---

12. Mandy draws a point on the number line. Which number belongs at the point?

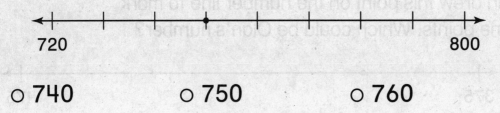

○ 740   ○ 750   ○ 760

Fill in the bubble for the correct answer.

1. Which number is shown?

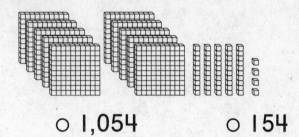

○ 1,045   ○ 1,054   ○ 154

2. Cassie made this model of the number 1,200.

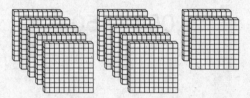

Which shows another way to model Cassie's number?

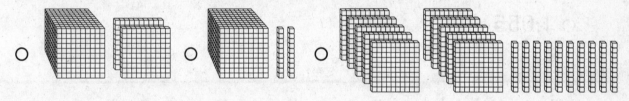

3. Chang uses blocks to model a number.

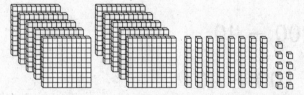

Which shows another way to model Chang's number?

GO ON

4. A number has 4 ones, 8 tens, 1 thousand, and no hundreds. Which is the number?

o 1,048

o 1,184

o 1,084

5. Kaley wrote a number this way. Which is the number?

$$1,000 + 50 + 5$$

o 1,050

o 1,155

o 1,055

6. Miley and her sister collect one thousand two hundred forty pennies. Which is another way to write this number?

o 1,000 + 200 + 40

o 100 + 200 + 40

o 1,000 + 100 + 40

GO ON

7. The number of people in Dana's town is less than 1,145. Which could be the number of people in Dana's town?

○ 1,182

○ 1,124

○ 1,151

8. Which number makes a true comparison?

$$1,115 < \underline{\hspace{2cm}}$$

○ 1,112   ○ 1,151   ○ 915

9. Which number makes a true comparison?

$$1,096 > \underline{\hspace{2cm}}$$

○ 1,178

○ 1,111

○ 1,043

GO ON

10. Which number makes a true comparison?

$$724 < \underline{\hspace{2cm}}$$

○ 1,064

○ 587

○ 699

---

11. Fran's Fruit Farm sells 973 oranges, 892 pears, and 1,025 apples. Which is the greatest number?

○ 973

○ 892

○ 1,025

---

12. Kiera collects sports cards. She has 1,121 basketball cards and 1,075 baseball cards. Which comparison is true?

○ 1,121 < 1,075

○ 1,075 < 1,121

○ 1,075 > 1,121

Fill in the bubble for the correct answer.

1. Nadia drew this shape. Which word describes the parts?

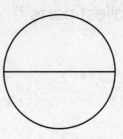

○ halves   ○ eighths   ○ fourths

---

2. Which word makes this sentence true?

   Square B has _____ equal parts than Square A.

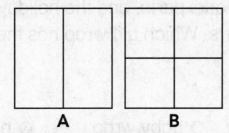

○ smaller   ○ fewer   ○ larger

---

3. Which word makes this sentence true?

   Circle B has _____ equal parts than Circle A.

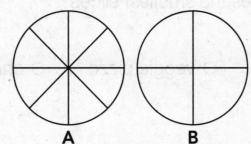

○ smaller   ○ more   ○ larger

GO ON ▶

4. Three sandwiches are the same size. The turkey sandwich is cut into halves. The tuna sandwich is cut into eighths. The roast beef sandwich is cut into fourths. Which is sandwich is cut into the smallest parts?

   ○ turkey sandwhich

   ○ roast beef sandwich

   ○ tuna sandwich

5. Lin has 3 sheets of gift wrap that are the same size. She cuts the birthday wrap into 4 equal parts, the baby wrap into 6 equal parts, and the holiday wrap into 12 equal parts. Which gift wrap has the largest parts?

   ○ birthday wrap   ○ baby wrap   ○ holiday wrap

6. Jaden makes 3 pizzas that are the same size. He cuts the cheese pizza into 4 equal slices, the veggie pizza into 12 equal slices, and the meat pizza into 8 equal slices. Which pizza has the smallest slices?

   ○ meat pizza   ○ veggie pizza   ○ cheese pizza

7. Maya drew this shape.

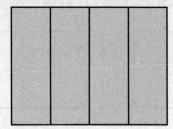

What amount of her shape is shaded?

○ I fourth   ○ 4 eighths   ○ 4 fourths

---

8. Which shape shows equal parts?

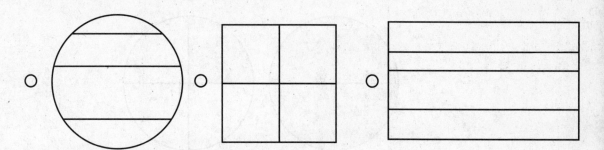

○   ○   ○

---

9. Which shape shows fourths?

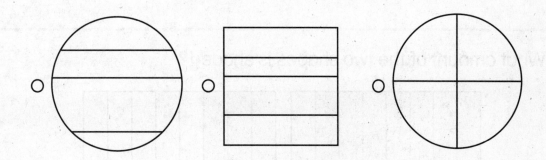

○   ○   ○

GO ON ➡

10. Brianna has two equal lengths of ribbon. She cuts each ribbon into sixths. She uses 8 pieces.

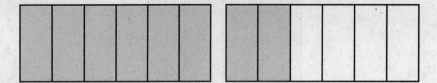

How much ribbon did she use?

○ one and 6 sixths   ○ one and 2 sixths   ○ 10 sixths

11. Forrester cuts two pancakes into fourths.

He eats 3 pieces and his friend eats 2 pieces.

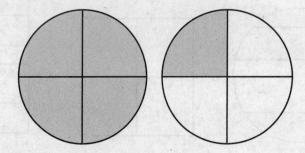

How much of the pancakes did they eat?

○ 2 fourths   ○ two wholes   ○ one and one fourth

12. What amount of the two shapes is shaded?

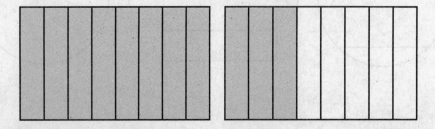

○ one and 3 eighths   ○ 2 eighths   ○ 1 eighth

Fill in the bubble for the correct answer.

1. On Monday, there were 7 boats in the pond.
   On Tuesday there were double that number.
   How many boats were in the pond on Tuesday?

   ○ 14

   ○ 7

   ○ 5

---

2. A fire truck has twice as many wheels as
   Lee's tricycle. His tricycle has 3 wheels.
   How many wheels does the fire truck have?

   ○ 3

   ○ 5

   ○ 6

---

3. Adam makes a ten to add $9 + 8$. What number
   should he write in the box?

   ○ 6

   ○ 7

   ○ 8

   $9 + 8$

   $9 + 1 + \blacksquare$

   $10 + \blacksquare = 17$

GO ON

4. Kelly has 7 tickets and Mica has 5 tickets for the fair. Which is a way to find how many tickets they have together?

○ $10 + 2$ ○ $10 + 5$ ○ $10 + 7$

---

5. Which addition fact can you use to find $14 - 8$?

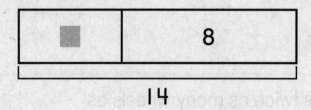

○ $8 + 7 = $ ■   ○ $6 + 8 = $ ■   ○ $6 + 7 = $ ■

---

6. Ella has a bag of 6 oranges and a bag of 8 oranges. Her math club eats 5 oranges. How many oranges does Ella have now?

○ 3   ○ 11   ○ 9

GO ON ➡

7. What tens fact can you use to find $15 - 7$?

○ $10 - 6 = 4$

○ $10 - 5 = 5$

○ $10 - 2 = 8$

---

8. Lana sang 11 songs in the first show and 6 songs in the second show. How many more songs did she sing in the first show than in the second show?

○ 5

○ 4

○ 17

---

9. On the playground, there are 4 boys playing catch and 6 girls jumping rope. There are 2 other boys playing tag. How many children are on the playground?

○ 10

○ 12

○ 6

GO ON

10. There are 6 boys and 9 girls watching a softball game. How many children are watching the softball game?

     ○ 14   ○ 17   ○ 15

---

11. Nestor and Will played basketball. Nestor won the game with 12 points. That was 6 points more than Will had. What number sentence shows how many points Will had?

     ○ $12 - 6 = 7$ ○ $12 + 6 = 18$ ○ $12 - 6 = 6$

---

12. Jose has some blue toy cars and 5 red toy cars. He has 14 toy cars altogether. Which number sentence shows how many blue toy cars Jose has?

     ○ $14 - 5 = 9$ ○ $14 + 5 = 19$ ○ $14 - 9 = 5$

STOP

Fill in the bubble for the correct answer.

1. The snack bar sold 8 pretzels on Friday and
   37 pretzels on Saturday. How many pretzels
   were sold in those two days?

   ○ 46

   ○ 35

   ◐ 45

---

2. Dena sells beads at a craft store. On Monday
   18 people buy beads. On Tuesday 5 people
   buy beads. How many people buy beads on
   the two days?

   ○ 23   ○ 22   ○ 21

---

3. Kitty scores 67 points in four frames of bowling.
   In the next frame she scores 7 more points.
   How many points did Kitty score?

   ○ 72   ○ 74   ○ 70

GO ON

4. Which shows how to add 48 + 33 by making one addend the next tens number?

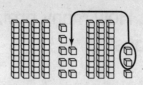

   ○ 50 + 30   ○ 50 + 31   ○ 50 + 33

---

5. There are 16 children in the water and 26 children on the beach. How many children are there?

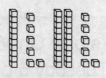

   ○ 52   ○ 42   ○ 45

---

6. Nadia has 17 crackers in one bag and 44 crackers in another bag. How many crackers does she have altogether?

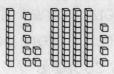

   ○ 51   ○ 60   ○ 61

GO ON ➤

7. What number goes in the box?

$$36 \longrightarrow 30 + 6$$
$$+ 48 \longrightarrow 40 + 8$$
$$\underline{70} + \underline{14} = \blacksquare$$

○ 84   ○ 74   ○ 56

---

8. Sheena has 13 crayons. She has 1 more crayon than Wally. How many crayons do Sheena and Wally have altogether?

○ 26

○ 14

○ 25

---

9. Glenn washed 27 cups. His father washed 45 cups. How many cups did they wash?

○ 82

○ 72

○ 71

GO ON

10. Kendra finds 47 shells at the beach. The next day she finds 16 shells. How many shells does Kendra find?

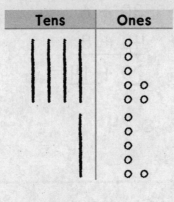

○ 63   ○ 53   ○ 62

---

11. Mr. Smith's students fly 19 kites. Ms. Baker's students fly 22 kites. Six kites fell down. How many kites were still flying?

○ 37   ○ 25   ○ 35

---

12. Justin and his friends make posters for a school play. They make 57 posters on Saturday and 34 posters on Sunday. How many posters did they make?

○ 91   ○ 80   ○ 81

STOP

Fill in the bubble for the correct answer.

1. Kai had 59 baseball cards. He bought 24 more. How many baseball cards does Kai have now?

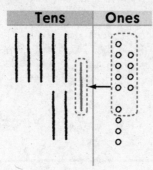

| Tens | Ones |

○ 73   ○ 82   ○ 83

---

2. Brody has 56 pennies. He spends 10 pennies. Then his father gives him 24 pennies. How many pennies does he have now?

○ 70 pennies

○ 34 pennies

○ 90 pennies

---

3. Max makes two picture frames. He glues 34 shells on one picture frame and 27 shells on the other picture frame. How many shells does Max use?

○ 51

○ 61

○ 60

GO ON →

4. Rob had 67 action figures in his collection.
He bought 15 more at a yard sale. How many
action figures does he have now?

○ 72

○ 55

○ 82

5. Mr. Wolf has 22 red pens, 16 black pens, and
26 blue pens. How many pens does he have?

○ 54

○ 64

○ 63

6. Charlie had 42 balloons. He bought 25 more
balloons. Then Brett gave him 36 balloons.
How many balloons does Charlie have now?

○ 103

○ 67

○ 93

GO ON

7. Patty picked 22 flowers. Kim picked 36 flowers.
Eddie picked 14 flowers and Mike picked 25 flowers.
How many flowers did the four children pick?

○ 97

○ 87

○ 72

8. Jill went to a library. She saw 23 boys and 20 girls reading.
She also saw 17 people listening to a storyteller and 42 people
using computers. How many people did Jill see?

○ 104

○ 111

○ 102

9. Ralph saw some dogs at a park. 17 of the dogs were
swimming in the lake and 19 were playing in the grass.
Which number sentence shows how many dogs Ralph saw?

○ $17 + \blacksquare = 19$

○ $17 + 19 = \blacksquare$

○ $\blacksquare + 17 = 19$

GO ON

10. Mary saw 16 muffins at the bakery. 12 of the muffins were banana and the rest were blueberry. Which number sentence shows how many muffins were blueberry?

   ○ 12 + ■ = 16

   ○ 12 + 16 = ■

   ○ 16 + ■ = 34

---

11. Jeff practiced batting. He made 14 hits. His friend made 18 hits. Which number sentence shows how many hits they made?

   ○ 18 + 18 = ■

   ○ ■ + 14 = 18

   ○ 14 + 18 = ■

---

12. Jena drew birds. She drew 12 birds in a tree and 16 birds flying in the sky. Which number sentence shows how many birds Jena drew?

   ○ 12 + 28 = ■

   ○ 12 + 16 = ■

   ○ ■ + 12 = 16

Fill in the bubble for the correct answer.

1. Abby uses blocks to show a number. She uses
9 ones blocks, 8 tens blocks, and 3 hundreds
blocks. What number does she show?

  ○ 893

  ○ 389

  ○ 983

2. What number is shown?

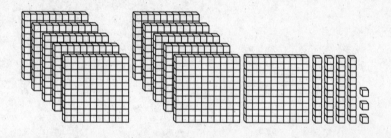

  ○ 1,043   ○ 1,143   ○ 1,053

3. What number is shown with these blocks?

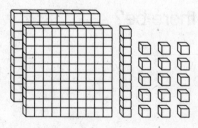

  ○ 215   ○ 235   ○ 225

GO ON

4. Which is another way to write 720?

o 600 + 20

o seven hundreds, 2 tens

o 70 + 2

5. A number has 2 ones, 6 tens, I thousand and no hundreds. What is the number?

o 1,026

o 1,162

o 1,062

6. There are 672 red roses in the garden. There are fewer yellow roses than red roses. How many yellow roses could there be?

o 1,000

o 574

o 674

GO ON

7. Which number makes the comparison true?

$$783 < 1,084 < \text{_____}$$

- ○ 1,098
- ○ 1,049
- ○ 898

8. Compare 848 and 488. Which of these is true?

- ○ 848 is greater than 488
- ○ 848 is equal to 488
- ○ 848 is less than 488

9. Compare 493 and 549. Which of these is true?

- ○ $493 < 549$
- ○ $493 = 549$
- ○ $493 > 549$

GO ON

10. Sam has 156 marbles. Zoe has 144 marbles.
Jim has 167 marbles. Compare their marbles.
Which of these is true?

   ○ 167 < 144 < 156

   ○ 167 < 156 < 144

   ○ 144 < 156 < 167

---

11. Nolan drew this shape. Which word describes the parts?

   ○ fourths

   ○ eighths

   ○ halves

---

12. Which word makes this sentence true?

Circle B has _____ equal parts than Circle A.

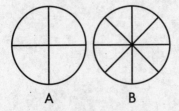

   ○ smaller   ○ fewer   ○ larger

GO ON ➡

13. Calvin has 3 sheets of paper that are the same size. He cuts the blue paper into 2 equal parts, the red paper into 4 equal parts, and the yellow paper into 8 equal parts. Which color of paper has the largest parts?

○ blue

○ red

○ yellow

14. What amount of the two shapes is shaded?

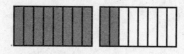

○ one eighth   ○ one and 2 eighths   ○ 6 eighths

15. Fran cuts two pizzas into sixths.

She eats 3 pieces and her brother eats 4 pieces.

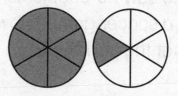

How many pizzas did they eat altogether?

○ 2 sixths   ○ two wholes   ○ one and one sixth

GO ON

16. There are 5 boys and 7 girls watching a play.
How many children are watching the play?

○ 11

○ 15

○ 12

---

17. Debbie works at a bakery. On Monday
16 people buy bread. On Tuesday 9 people
buy bread. How many people buy bread?

○ 25

○ 24

○ 23

---

18. Jack went to a park. He saw 22 boys and 19 girls
at the petting zoo. He saw 20 people fishing and
41 people watching a soccer game. How many
people did Jack see at the park?

○ 102

○ 112

○ 92

Fill in the bubble for the correct answer.

1. On Thursday, it rained for 7 hours. There
   are 24 hours in a full day. How many hours was
   it dry on Thursday?

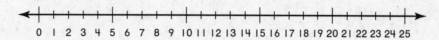

0 1 2 3 4 5 6 7 8 9 10 11 12 13 14 15 16 17 18 19 20 21 22 23 24 25

   ○ 14

   ○ 16

   ○ 17

2. Break apart ones to subtract 63 − 8. What number
   goes in the box?

$$63 - 8 = \blacksquare$$
$$\underset{3 \quad 5}{\wedge}$$

   ○ 55   ○ 65   ○ 71

3. Kim and Carl saw 31 birds fishing at the beach.
   Then 8 birds flew away. How many birds are left
   fishing at the beach?

   ○ 33

   ○ 23

   ○ 12

GO ON ➤

4. There are 66 children at a playground. Then
   18 of the children leave. How many children are
   still at the playground?

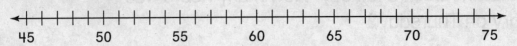

45   50   55   60   65   70   75

○ 46

○ 50

○ 48

5. Break apart ones to subtract 42 − 18. What number
   goes in the box?

$$42 - 18 = \blacksquare$$

10   8

2   6

○ 32   ○ 24   ○ 26

6. There are 42 plates in the first stack. There are
   17 plates in the second stack. How many more
   plates are in the first stack than in the second stack?

○ 25

○ 35

○ 59

GO ON

7. Mrs. Blum has a box of 45 paintbrushes.
   She gives 16 paintbrushes to her students.
   How many paintbrushes does Mrs. Blum have now?

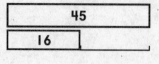

   ○ 29   ○ 61   ○ 27

8. There are 84 crackers in the box. Ed and Darius
   each take 16 crackers out of the box. How many
   crackers are in the box now?

   ○ 62

   ○ 68

   ○ 52

9. There are 63 red beads in a jar at the bead store.
   During the day customers bought 18 of the red beads.
   How many red beads are left in the jar?

   ○ 55

   ○ 71

   ○ 45

   GO ON ➜

10. Lee sees 27 grasshoppers. Ally sees 9 grasshoppers. How many fewer grasshoppers does Ally see than Lee?

○ 18

○ 8

○ 22

11. Lucy had 58 crackers in a bag. She gave 36 crackers to first graders. How many crackers does she have left?

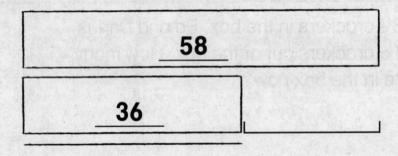

○ 16   ○ 12   ○ 22

12. Rosa sees 3 goats in a pen. She sees 37 more goats go into the pen. Then she sees 14 goats leave the pen. How many goats are left in the pen?

○ 23

○ 26

○ 34

Fill in the bubble for the correct answer.

1. There are 38 buttons in a box. If Stella uses 19 for a craft project, how many buttons will still be in the box?

  ○ 19

  ○ 57

  ○ 48

2. Kevin had 53 rocks. He gave 17 to his sister. How many rocks does he have now?

  ○ 70

  ○ 36

  ○ 48

3. Suri had 46 pennies. She gave 14 to her sister. How many pennies does she have now?

  ○ 60

  ○ 50

  ○ 32

GO ON

4. There are 46 horses in a field. Of these, 24 are brown and the rest are black. Which number sentence can you use to find how many horses are black?

   ○ $46 + 24 = $ ■

   ○ $46 - 22 = $ ■

   ○ $46 - 24 = $ ■

5. There are 34 birds on a fence. Of these, 19 are blue and the rest are red. Which number sentence can you use to find how many birds are red?

   ○ $34 + 19 = $ ■

   ○ $34 - 19 = $ ■

   ○ $34 - 15 = $ ■

6. Tina picks 21 lemons. Matt picks 4 more lemons than Tina picks. How many lemons do the two children pick?

   ○ 46

   ○ 17

   ○ 25

GO ON

7. Debbie collects toy bugs. She has 22 toy spiders.
She has 9 more toy butterflies than spiders.
How many toy bugs does Debbie have?

○ 13

○ 31

○ 53

---

8. Tyson took 34 photos of his pets. His dad took
6 more photos of the pets than Tyson took.
How many photos did Tyson and his dad take altogether?

○ 74

○ 38

○ 28

---

9. Tameka made 32 banana muffins. She made
24 apple muffins. She gave 12 of her muffins to her
neighbors. How many muffins does she have now?

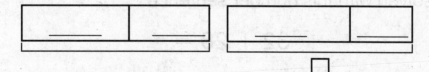

○ 20

○ 44

○ 12

GO ON ▶

10. Bonnie picked 23 green peppers. She picked 35 tomatoes. She sold 15 of the vegetables at the farmer's market. How many vegetables does she have now?

○ 38

○ 43

○ 8

---

11. Terry has a box of 24 baseball cards. Which problem can be solved with this number sentence?

$$60 - 24 = \blacksquare$$

○ What is the total number of baseball cards Terry will have if he gets 60 more?

○ How many more cards does Terry need to have 60 baseball cards?

○ How many cards will Terry have if he buys 24 more cards?

---

12. Dana has a bag of 32 stickers. Which problem can be solved with this number sentence?

$$32 + 28 = \blacksquare$$

○ What is the total number of stickers Dana will have if she gives 28 to her friend?

○ How many stickers will Dana have if her friend gives her 28 more stickers?

○ How many stickers will Dana have if she buys 4 more stickers?

Fill in the bubble for the correct answer.

1. There are 417 children visiting the Science Center. There are 226 children visiting the Art Center. How many children are visiting the two centers?

   ○ 643

   ○ 633

   ○ 725

2. On Saturday, 165 tickets were sold for the play. On Sunday, 218 tickets were sold. How many tickets were sold on both days?

   ○ 273

   ○ 383

   ○ 373

3. There are 355 pears packed in boxes. There are 263 pears packed in baskets. How many pears are there in the boxes and baskets?

   ○ 618   ○ 518   ○ 608

4. Mrs. Lopez had 250 bottles of water.
She sold 123 bottles of water at
the ball field. How many bottles of
water does she have now?

- ○ 123

- ○ 127

- ○ 373

5. Mr. Franklin has 274 badges. He gives
133 badges to some sports teams.
How many badges does he still have?

- ○ 131

- ○ 147

- ○ 141

6. Jason wants to build a birdhouse
with craft sticks. He needs 235
craft sticks to build the birdhouse.
He has 163 craft sticks. How many
more craft sticks does he need
for the birdhouse?

- ○ 132

- ○ 72

- ○ 398

7. There are 436 board games and 350 video
games at a toy store. The store gets more
video games. Now the store has 947 games.
How many more video games did the store get?

    ○ 241   ○ 161   ○ 786

8. There are 386 people hiking
on a trail. 223 people reach the
end of the trail. How many people
are still hiking?

    ○ 163

    ○ 173

    ○ 609

9. Joe's snack stand has 360 juice boxes.
Joe sells 234 juice boxes one week.
The next week he sells 112 more
juice boxes. How many juice boxes
does Joe's snack stand have left?

    ○ 20

    ○ 14

    ○ 126

GO ON

10. On Thursday, 137 people went to a zoo. On Friday, 239 people went to the zoo. On Saturday, 499 people went to the zoo. Which number sentence can be used to find the number of people that went to the zoo on Thursday and Saturday?

   ○ $137 + 239 = \blacksquare$

   ○ $499 - 137 = \blacksquare$

   ○ $499 + 137 = \blacksquare$

11. There are 216 people watching a parade. Then 372 more people come to watch. Which number sentence can be used to find the number of people watching the parade now?

   ○ $372 - 216 = \blacksquare$

   ○ $372 + 216 = \blacksquare$

   ○ $216 + \blacksquare = 372$

12. The are 514 fans at the baseball field on Monday and 426 fans on Tuesday. Which number sentence can be used to find the number of fans at the baseball field on both days?

   ○ $514 - 426 = \blacksquare$

   ○ $426 + \blacksquare = 514$

   ○ $514 + 426 = \blacksquare$

Fill in the bubble for the correct answer.

1. Abby is at the bowling alley. She buys
   a bag of pretzels. She uses these coins.
   How much do the pretzels cost?

○ 80¢   ○ 50¢   ○ 85¢

---

2. Ed puts these coins in his coin bank.
   How much money does he put in the bank?

○ 40¢   ○ 35¢   ○ 20¢

---

3. Kathy gives these coins to her uncle.
   How much money does Kathy give
   to her uncle?

○ 75¢   ○ 35¢   ○ 65¢

GO ON

4. Linda gives Gabby these coins.
Which is the total value of the coins?

○ 22¢   ○ 47¢   ○ 37¢

---

5. Greg and Pedro have these coins.
Which is the total value of the coins?

○ 63¢   ○ 73¢   ○ 48¢

---

6. Jane puts these coins in a vending machine.
How much money does Jane put in the machine?

○ 65¢   ○ 45¢   ○ 55¢

GO ON ➡

7. Melissa has one dollar. She writes the total value as 100¢. Which is another way to write one dollar?

○ $100

○ $1.00

○ 1¢

8. Ira has 63¢. Which is another way to write the amount of money that Ira has?

○ $63

○ 0.63¢

○ $0.63

9. Ali has these coins. Which is the total value of the coins?

○ $1.00

○ 10¢

○ 1¢

GO ON ➤

10. Ellen uses 1 quarter, 1 dime, and 2 nickels to buy a stamp. How much does the stamp cost?

○ $0.45

○ $0.40

○ $0.35

11. Aisha has 1 dime, 2 nickels, and 2 quarters. She wants to buy a banana for 50¢. How much money will she have after she buys the banana?

○ $0.25

○ $0.10

○ $0.20

12. Umi uses 2 quarters, 3 dimes, and 5 pennies to buy an apple. How much does the apple cost?

○ $0.55

○ $0.40

○ $0.85

Fill in the bubble for the correct answer.

1. Ava has 5 bags of toys. She has 3 toys in each bag. How many toys does she have?

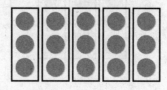

    ○ 15   ○ 8   ○ 18

2. Keri sees some bikes in a bike rack. Which sentence best describes what she sees?

    ○ She sees 3 bikes that have 5 tires each.

    ○ She sees 3 bikes that have 2 tires each.

    ○ She sees 5 bikes that have 2 tires each.

3. Which sentence best describes the picture?

    ○ 4 children with 3 counters each.

    ○ 4 children with 4 counters each.

    ○ 7 children with 2 counters each.

GO ON

4. There are 3 kittens in a basket. Each kitten has 4 feet. How many feet are there?

○ 3   ○ 12   ○ 7

---

5. Gino has 6 plates. He puts 3 pancakes on each plate. How many pancakes are on the plates?

○ 9   ○ 12   ○ 18

---

6. Sasha buys 1 box of peanut butter crackers. The box has 32 crackers. She shares the crackers equally with 4 friends. How many crackers does each friend get?

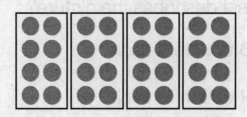

○ 12   ○ 3   ○ 8

GO ON ➡

7. Otto has 24 fruit bars. He places the same number of fruit bars in 8 bags. How many fruit bars are in each bag?

    ○ 3   ○ 8   ○ 6

---

8. There are 14 kites. Each child gets 2 kites. How many children are there?

    ○ 7

    ○ 5

    ○ 4

---

9. Which sentence best describes the picture?

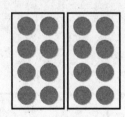

    ○ 10 pens are divided into 2 groups.

    ○ 16 pens are divided into 2 groups.

    ○ 8 pens are divided into 2 groups.

GO ON

10. Toby has 28 markers. He divides them into 4 equal groups. How many markers are in each group?

    ○ 32

    ○ 4

    ○ 7

11. Elena has 18 biscuits. She places an equal number of biscuits on each of 2 pans. How many biscuits are on each pan?

    ○ 9

    ○ 20

    ○ 16

12. The audience sits in chairs to watch the play. There are 6 equal rows of chairs. There are 48 chairs. How many chairs are in each row?

    ○ 40

    ○ 8

    ○ 24

Fill in the bubble for the correct answer.

1. Yesterday, it rained for 6 hours.
   There are 24 hours in a day.
   How many hours was it dry?

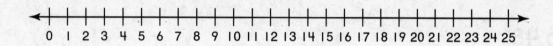

   ○ 15 hours   ○ 18 hours   ○ 16 hours

2. There are 235 bags of beans on shelves.
   There are 375 bags of beans packed in
   boxes. How many bags of beans are
   there on shelves and in boxes?

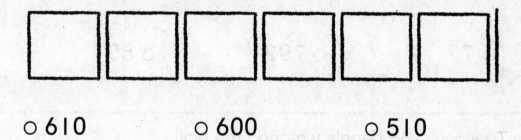

   ○ 610   ○ 600   ○ 510

3. There are 48 guppies in a tank at the pet shop.
   Of these, 22 guppies have yellow tails and the
   rest have red tails. How many of the guppies have red tails?

   ○ 25

   ○ 70

   ○ 26

GO ON

4. Jake picks 22 flowers. Diego picks 4 more than Jake. How many flowers do the children pick?

○ 26

○ 48

○ 18

5. There are 432 shirts with short sleeves and 360 shirts with long sleeves in a store. The store gets more long-sleeve shirts. Now the store has 842 shirts. How many more shirts did the store get?

○ 72   ○ 792   ○ 50

6. On Tuesday, 135 people watched the play.
On Wednesday, 233 people watched the play.
On Thursday, 423 people watched the play.
Which number sentence can be used to find the number of people that watched the play on Tuesday and Thursday?

○ $135 + 233 = $ ■

○ $423 - 135 = $ ■

○ $135 + 423 = $ ■

GO ON

7. Angel is at the movies. She buys a drink. She uses these coins. Which is the value of the coins she uses?

  ○ 85¢   ○ 90¢   ○ 95¢

8. David puts these coins in his pocket. Which is the value of the coins he puts in his pocket?

  ○ 20¢   ○ 40¢   ○ 55¢

9. Mandy has 100 pennies in a jar. She writes the total value of her pennies as 100¢. Which is another way to write the total value?

  ○ $1.00

  ○ $100

  ○ 1¢

GO ON ➤

10. Alex has 1 dime, 2 nickels, and 2 quarters. He wants to buy an orange for 60¢. How much money will he have after he buys the orange?

   ○ 20¢   ○ 10¢   ○ 60¢

---

11. Harry has 4 packages of gum. There are 5 sticks in each package. How many sticks of gum does he have?

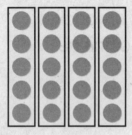

   ○ 20   ○ 9   ○ 15

---

12. Calvin saw some dogs in a pond. There were 5 dogs. Which sentence best describes what he saw?

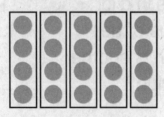

○ He saw 4 dogs that have 5 legs each.

○ He saw 5 dogs that have 4 legs each.

○ He saw 4 dogs that have 4 legs each.

GO ON ➡

13. Which sentence best describes the picture?

○ 3 puppies with 4 legs each.

○ 4 puppies with 4 legs each.

○ 7 puppies with 4 legs each.

---

14. Amir has 4 plates. He puts 5 bagels
on each plate. How many bagels
are on the plates?

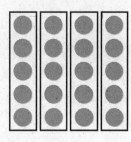

○ 9   ○ 16   ○ 20

---

15. Elsa has a bowl of 18 boiled eggs. She shares
the boiled eggs so that she and 5 friends get the
same number. How many boiled eggs does
each person get?

○ 3   ○ 12   ○ 6

GO ON ➡

16. Karl and his 2 brothers read books. Which sentence best describes what they read?

○ The 3 brothers read 5 books.

○ The 3 brothers read 3 books.

○ The 2 brothers read 3 books.

---

17. Vicky has 15 sweet potato pies. She places the same number of pies on each of 3 shelves. How many pies are on each shelf?

○ 5

○ 12

○ 18

---

18. The parents sit in rows of stadium seats to watch baseball practice. There are 4 rows of stadium seats with the same number in each row. If there are 28 seats, how many seats are in each row?

○ 32   ○ 7   ○ 24

STOP

Fill in the bubble for the correct answer.

1. There are an even number of bunnies and
   an odd number of gerbils in the pet store.
   Which could be the number of bunnies
   and gerbils?

   ○ 11 bunnies and 6 gerbils

   ○ 12 bunnies and 7 gerbils

   ○ 13 bunnies and 6 gerbils

2. There are 165 buttons in Felix's bag. The number
   of buttons in Mary's bag is 10 less than 165.
   How many buttons are in Mary's bag?

   ○ 175

   ○ 155

   ○ 166

3. Marina took 132 photos. Jordan took 10 more
   photos than Marina. How many photos did
   Jordan take?

   ○ 122

   ○ 132

   ○ 142

4. Mica has 10 more shells than Julie. Julie has 67 shells. The number of shells Fay has is 10 less than the number Mica has. How many shells does Fay have?

○ 77

○ 67

○ 57

5. Pete gives 10 balloons to children each week. After six weeks, he has 175 balloons. He gives 10 more balloons to children the next week. How many balloons does he have now?

○ 174

○ 165

○ 185

6. There are 386 crayons in a basket. There are 100 fewer crayons in the closet. How many crayons are in the closet?

○ 376

○ 486

○ 286

GO ON

7. Toby and Scott build a tower with
238 blocks. Then, the tower falls over and
100 blocks fall down. How many
blocks are left in the tower?

○ 138

○ 338

○ 237

8. Sandy's collection has 395 coins.
She puts 100 coins in special cases.
How many coins are not in cases yet?

○ 495

○ 95

○ 295

9. There are 260 children on the soccer field
on Saturday morning. Then, 100 more children
arrive at the soccer field. How many
children are on the soccer field now?

○ 270

○ 360

○ 160

GO ON

10. Candy and Mandy catch 12 tadpoles in all.
    Candy catches 7 tadpoles. How many tadpoles
    does Mandy catch?

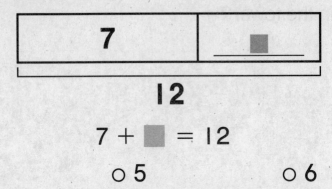

$$7 + \blacksquare = 12$$

    ○ 19   ○ 5   ○ 6

11. Jada has some markers. Heather has
    12 markers. They have 36 markers altogether.
    How many markers does Jada have?

    ○ 24   ○ 23   ○ 48

12. Tomas painted 32 paw prints on a dog bowl. Misty
    painted 14 more paw prints on the dog bowl.
    What number sentence can be used to find the
    number of paw prints painted on the dog bowl?

  ○ $32 - 14 = \blacksquare$

  ○ $32 + 14 = \blacksquare$

  ○ $14 + \blacksquare = 44$

GO ON ➡

13. There are 34 bricks in a box. There are
    39 bricks in a wheelbarrow. How many
    bricks are there?

    ○ 73

    ○ 75

    ○ 63

14. Dena's class has two boxes of solid shapes.
    The first box has 25 solid shapes. The second
    box has 36 solid shapes. How many solid
    shapes are in the two boxes?

    ○ 56

    ○ 51

    ○ 61

15. Mr. Bell's class has 21 children. Some of the
    children were drawing pictures and the rest
    of the children were making clay models.
    If 18 children were making clay models,
    how many children were drawing pictures?

    ○ 3

    ○ 13

    ○ 6

GO ON

16. Kam has a jar with 230 marbles. She gives
    103 to her brother. How many marbles does
    Kam have now?

    ○ 126

    ○ 127

    ○ 333

17. Vilma put 45 stars on her window. Ron put
    15 more stars on his window than Vilma. Which
    number sentence can be used to find the
    number of stars that Ron put on his window?

    ○ 45 + 15 = ▨

    ○ 45 − 15 = ▨

    ○ 15 + ▨ = 45

18. Mr. Muschamp has 67 posters in his office and
    48 posters in the library. There are fish on
    12 posters. How many posters do not have
    fish on them?

    ○ 115

    ○ 103

    ○ 36

Fill in the bubble for the correct answer.

1. Anna draws this shape. How many vertices does her shape have?

○ 8 vertices   ○ 7 vertices   ○ 6 vertices

2. Li drew two-dimensional shapes with 16 sides in all. Which shapes could Li have drawn?

○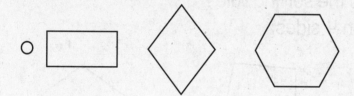

○

○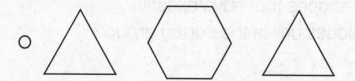

3. Harrison drew this hexagon. How many vertices does a hexagon have?

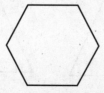

○ 5 vertices   ○ 4 vertices   ○ 6 vertices   **GO ON**

4. How many sides does this polygon have?

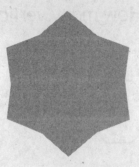

○ 12 sides   ○ 11 sides   ○ 10 sides

---

5. Which shape matches the sorting rule?
   Shapes with more than 4 sides

○ 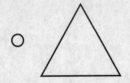   ○    ○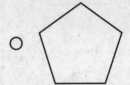

---

6. Zach sorts a group of shapes that have exactly
   3 sides. How many shapes are in the sorted group?

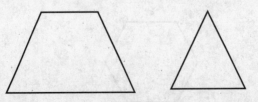

○ 5   ○ 3   ○ 2

GO ON ➡

7. Mia sorts a group of shapes that have exactly
6 vertices. How many shapes are in the sorted group?

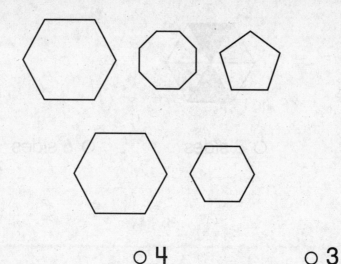

○ 5   ○ 4   ○ 3

8. Vinnie put two blocks together to make a new shape
with 8 sides. Which two blocks did Vinnie use?

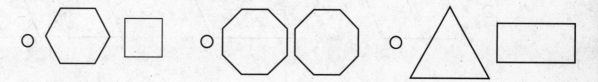

9. Ella put three blocks together to make a new shape.
How many vertices does her new shape have?

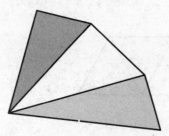

○ 5 vertices   ○ 6 vertices   ○ 7 vertices

GO ON

10. Beth put these blocks together to make a new shape. How many sides does her new shape have?

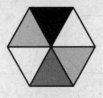

○ 10 sides   ○ 8 sides   ○ 6 sides

11. Which shows a way to fold and cut a quadrilateral to make two triangles?

○    ○    ○

12. Mike folds this shape along the lines. What new shapes does he make?

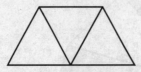

○ triangles   ○ trapezoids   ○ quadrilaterals

Name _____

Fill in the bubble for the correct answer.

1. Which object matches the shape of a sphere?

○ 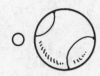   ○   ○

---

2. Which of these solids is a cylinder?

○ 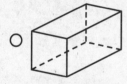   ○   ○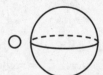

---

3. Which of these solids rolls?

○ 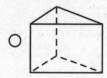   ○ 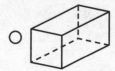   ○

GO ON

4. Ryan puts his shoes in a box. The box has
2 square faces and 4 rectangular faces.
Which is the name for the box?

○ rectangular prism

○ triangular prism

○ cylinder

5. Barbara has a solid block. Her block has
6 faces, 12 edges, and 8 vertices.
Which solid does Barbara have?

○ cone

○ cube

○ triangular prism

6. Which solid has six faces?

○ triangular prism

○ cone

○ cube

7. Carla has a block that is a triangular prism. How many vertices does a triangular prism have?

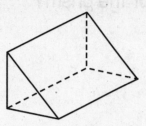

○ 5 vertices   ○ 9 vertices   ○ 6 vertices

8. Starla built a rectangular prism using unit cubes. How many unit cubes did Starla use?

○ 12   ○ 14   ○ 16

9. Look at the top, side, and front views of Sue's rectangular prism. How many unit cubes did Sue use to build it?

top view   front view   side view

○ 20 unit cubes   ○ 24 unit cubes   ○ 26 unit cubes

GO ON

10. Rene builds the first layer of a rectangular prism using 8 cubes. She adds another layer of cubes. How many cubes are used for the prism?

   ○ 6

   ○ 10

   ○ 16

---

11. Sam builds the first layer of a rectangular prism using 12 cubes. He adds 2 more layers. How many cubes are used for the prism?

   ○ 15

   ○ 24

   ○ 36

---

12. Etta builds the first layer of a rectangular prism using 10 cubes. She adds another layer of cubes. How many cubes are used for the prism?

   ○ 20

   ○ 12

   ○ 10

Fill in the bubble for the correct answer.

1. Jonah used color tiles to measure a straw.
   Which is the best choice for the length of the straw?

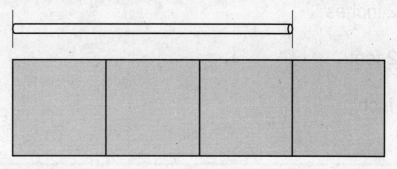

   ○ about 3 inches   ○ about 2 inches   ○ about 1 inch

---

2. Large paper clip chains are 12 inches long.
   Small paper clip chains are 5 inches long.
   Which shows how many paper clip chains are
   needed to have 29 inches of paper clip chains?

   ○ 1 large ⊂⊃ chain and 3 small ⊂⊃ chains

   ○ 2 large ⊂⊃ chains and 1 small ⊂⊃ chain

   ○ 1 large ⊂⊃ chain and 2 small ⊂⊃ chains

---

3. Stacey uses a ruler to measure a large paper clip.
   It is 2 inches long. Which sentence is true about
   the length of the paper clip?

   ○ 2 inches is the same as 2 feet.

   ○ 2 feet is a greater length than 2 inches.

   ○ 2 inches is a greater length than 2 feet.

4. Kai measures the length of a book. He says the book measures 1 foot. Which is the same length as 1 foot?

    ○ 12 inches

    ○ 12 feet

    ○ 1 inch

5. Use an inch ruler. What is the length of the crayon to the nearest inch?

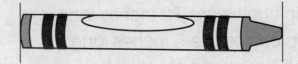

    ○ 2 inches

    ○ 3 inches

    ○ 1 inch

6. Bonnie chooses an object that is about 3 inches long. Which object did Bonnie choose?

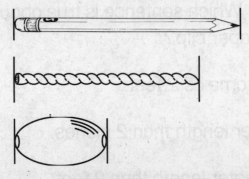

    ○ string   ○ pencil   ○ bead

GO ON

7. Craig needs 4 pieces of wood that are each about a foot long. Which length of wood will be closest to the amount he needs?

○ 36 inches long

○ 60 inches long

○ 48 inches long

8. Louella makes curtains that are about the same length as the ceiling to the floor. About how long are Louella's curtains?

○ about 7 feet long

○ about 7 inches long

○ about 2 feet long

9. Tyler has a toy racetrack set. Each piece of track is about 4 inches long. If Tyler puts 6 pieces of track together, about how long in feet, will the racetrack be?

○ about 2 feet

○ about 3 feet

○ about 10 feet

10. Each section of a bulletin board is 3 feet long.
Betty has some yarn. Betty's yarn is about
as long as 4 sections of bulletin board. Which
is the best estimate of Betty's yarn?

○ about 12 inches

○ about 40 inches

○ about 12 feet

11. Perry has a white shelf that is about 2 feet long.
He has a black shelf that is about half as long as
the white shelf. Which is the best estimate for
the length of the black shelf?

○ about 4 feet

○ about 10 inches

○ about 20 inches

12. Tanya has two paintbrushes. If the top paintbrush is
6 inches long, about how long is the bottom paintbrush?

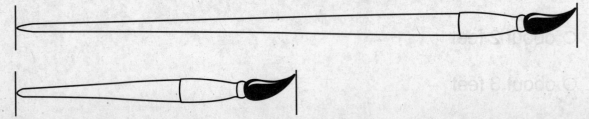

○ about 3 inches   ○ about 6 inches   ○ about 1 foot

Fill in the bubble for the correct answer.

1. Andy has a feather that he measures in centimeters. He draws this diagram to show its length. How many centimeters long is his feather?

○ 20 centimeters   ○ 23 centimeters   ○   25 centimeters

2. Julie has a piece of yarn that she measures in centimeters. She draws the diagram below to show its length. How long is her yarn?

○ 17 centimeters   ○ 18 centimeters   ○ 24 centimeters

3. Eve has 3 ribbons that are each 6 centimeters long. How many centimeters of ribbon does Eve have?

○ 20 centimeters

○ 19 centimeters

○ 18 centimeters

4. Keiki has a piece of wire that is 22 centimeters long. She uses 8 centimeters of it for a project. Then she uses 7 more centimeters of the wire for another project. How long is the wire that Keiki has left?

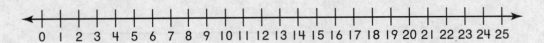

 ○ 7 centimeters   ○ 8 centimeters   ○ 9 centimeters

---

5. Use a centimeter ruler. Alyson has this pen. How long is the pen?

 ○ 8 centimeters   ○ 10 centimeters   ○ 11 centimeters

---

6. Use a centimeter ruler. Which is the best choice for the length of this paper clip?

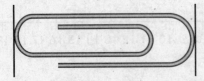

 ○ 5 centimeters   ○ 4 centimeters   ○ 7 centimeters

GO ON

7. Which is the best choice for the height of a rocket you would see at a space center?

○ 27 centimeters   ○ 27 meters   ○ 7 centimeters

8. Use a centimeter ruler. Which is the best choice for the length of the marker?

○ 10 centimeters

○ 11 centimeters

○ 1 centimeter

9. Ashton uses color tiles to make a rectangle. He uses 6 rows of tiles and 6 columns of tiles. How many tiles does Ashton use?

○ 12

○ 66

○ 36

GO ON

10. Mel puts color tiles on a table for a matching game. She puts the color tiles in 3 columns and 5 rows. How many color tiles does Mel put on the table?

  ○ 8

  ○ 15

  ○ 16

11. Harry uses color tiles to make a rectangle. There are 6 rows and 3 columns in his shape. How many color tiles cover the shape?

  ○ 18

  ○ 9

  ○ 3

12. Ali has 14 color tiles. He wants to make a rectangle with 7 rows and 3 columns. How many more color tiles does Ali need?

  ○ 6

  ○ 7

  ○ 11

Fill in the bubble for the correct answer.

1. Which object matches the shape of a rectangular prism?

   ○   ○   ○

---

2. Dan plays in a tent. The tent has 2 triangular faces and 3 rectangular faces. Which is the name for the tent?

   ○ triangular prism

   ○ rectangular prism

   ○ cylinder

---

3. Harrison drew this quadrilateral. How many vertices does a quadrilateral have?

   ○ 6

   ○ 5

   ○ 4

GO ON

4. How many sides does this polygon have?

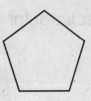

○ 5   ○ 6   ○ 8

---

5. Li sorts some shapes and makes a group of shapes that have exactly 4 vertices. How many shapes are in the group Li makes?

○ 5   ○ 4   ○ 2

---

6. Elena put two blocks together to make a new shape. How many vertices does her new shape have?

○ 4   ○ 5   ○ 7

GO ON ➡

7. Vic put two blocks together to make a new shape with 6 sides. Which two blocks did Vic use?

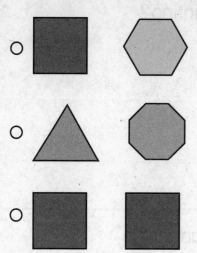

○

○

○

8. Steena built this rectangular prism using unit cubes. How many unit cubes did Steena use?

○ 8   ○ 10   ○ 12

9. Look at the top, side, and front views of Sid's rectangular prism. How many unit cubes did Sid use to build it?

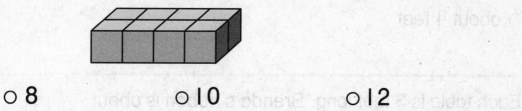

top view   front view   side view

○ 5   ○ 10   ○ 12

GO ON

10. Liz painted a picture on paper that is about the same length as the distance from the top of the door to the floor. About how long is Liz's painting?

○ about 6 feet

○ about 3 inches

○ about 6 inches

---

11. Toby has a train set. Each piece of track is about 6 inches long. If Toby puts 4 pieces of track together, about how long will the train track be in feet?

○ about 10 feet

○ about 2 feet

○ about 4 feet

---

12. Each table is 3 feet long. Brenda's ribbon is about as long as 3 tables. Which is the best estimate for the length of Brenda's ribbon?

○ about 9 inches

○ about 33 inches

○ about 9 feet

GO ON

13. Grace has two markers. If the gray marker is
6 inches long, about how long is the white marker?

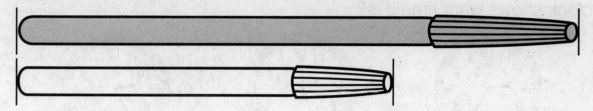

   ○ about 4 inches

   ○ about 2 inches

   ○ about 4 feet

---

14. Ron has 20 color tiles. He wants to use them to make
a rectangle with 4 rows and 6 columns of color tiles.
How many more color tiles does Ron need?

   ○ 5

   ○ 6

   ○ 4

---

15. Keri is going to the park at 10:15. Which clock shows
this time?

○    ○    ○

GO ON ➡

16. The hour hand points between the 9 and the 10.
In 25 minutes it will be the next hour. Which
clock shows what time it is?

○    ○    ○

17. Jared's class went to the library when lunch
ended. The clock shows when lunch ended.
What time did Jared's class go to the library?

○ 10:15 A.M.   ○ 11:15 A.M.   ○ 10:45 P.M.

18. Greg starts playing soccer at the time shown on
the clock. What time did he start playing soccer?

○ 5:02 P.M.   ○ 2:15 P.M.   ○ 2:15 A.M.

Name _____

Fill in the bubble for the correct answer.

1. Marta earns 5 dollars each week. She saves all of the money. How long will it take her to save 25 dollars?

   ○ 4 weeks

   ○ 5 weeks

   ○ 15 weeks

2. Felix earns 4 dollars a week. Each week he spends 2 dollars and saves the rest. How much money will he have in 4 weeks?

   ○ $8

   ○ $16

   ○ $12

3. Rhonda saves 7 dollars each month. How much will she save in 5 months?

   ○ 12 dollars

   ○ 28 dollars

   ○ 35 dollars

4. Carla gets one dime each week for 9 weeks.
   She saves 6 dimes and spends 3 dimes.
   How much money does she have now?

○ 30¢   ○ 60¢   ○ 90¢

5. Andre had these coins. He spends 20¢ and
   saves the rest. How much money does he save?

○ 65¢   ○ 55¢   ○ 45¢

6. Lon earns 75¢ each week. He wants to buy
   a stamp that costs 50¢. After two weeks
   he buys the stamp and saves the rest.
   How much money does he save?

○ $1.00   ○ 75¢   ○ 50¢

GO ON

7. Jessica has $18 in the bank. She makes a withdrawal of $5. How much does Jessica have in the bank now?

   ○ $23

   ○ $12

   ○ $13

8. Logan has $8 in the bank. He makes a withdrawal of $4. Later he deposits $6. How much money does Logan have in the bank now?

   ○ $8

   ○ $18

   ○ $10

9. Mrs. Good has $64 in the bank. She makes a deposit of $12. How much does Mrs. Good have in the bank now?

   ○ $66

   ○ $76

   ○ $52

GO ON

10. Jake has 63¢. He wants to buy a toy that costs 95¢. How much money does he need to borrow?

○ 32¢

○ 42¢

○ 36¢

11. Sophia has 89¢. She wants to buy crayons that cost 98¢. How much money does she need to borrow?

○ 187¢

○ 19¢

○ 9¢

12. Anthony has 49¢. He wants to buy a sticker that costs 65¢. How much money does he need to borrow?

○ 26¢

○ 16¢

○ 6¢

13. Ron lends $6 to Jake. Jake plans to pay $3 to Ron each week. How long will it take Jake to pay back all of the money?

○ 9 weeks

○ 3 weeks

○ 2 weeks

14. Aiden lends some money to Wendy. Wendy gives Aiden $3 each week for 5 weeks to pay back the money. How much did Aiden lend to Wendy?

○ $15

○ $2

○ $8

15. Kyra lends $12 to Jasmine. Jasmine plans to pay $3 to Kyra each week. How long will it take for Jasmine to pay back the $12?

○ 4 weeks

○ 9 weeks

○ 15 weeks

16. Mr. Hsing makes a painting. He sells the painting to Mr. Baker for $15. Who is the consumer?

○ Mr. Baker

○ Mr. Hsing

○ Both Mr. Baker and Mr. Hsing

17. Gabe has 95¢. He spends 25¢ on decals and 50¢ on wood to make a toy airplane. He sells the toy airplane to Lisa for 95¢. How much money does he have now?

○ $1.15

○ 95¢

○ 75¢

18. Miss Summers has $45. She spends $12 on supplies to make a pair of mittens. She sells the mittens for $18. How much money does she have now?

○ $33

○ $43

○ $51

Child's Name _____ Date _____

Prerequisite Skills Inventory

Item	Lesson	TEKS*	Common Error	Intervene with RtI* Tier 1 Lessons	Soar to Success Math
1	1.8	1.2.C	May confuse the hundreds, tens, and ones places	8	2.16
2	2.4	1.2.D	May confuse greater than and less than	9	7.18
3	2.5	1.2.F	May confuse the meaning of least and greatest	10	35.10
4	2.3	1.2.G	May not know the difference between > and <	13	7.15
5	5.4	1.3.B	May interpret the picture incorrectly	23	11.11
6	4.7	1.3.C	May not understand how to add without models	26	10.14
7	8.2	1.3.F	May not understand how the addition sentence relates to the situation	46	10.17
8	9.1	1.4.A	May confuse a nickel with a dime	48	3.09
9	9.2	1.4.C	May count by fives for all of the coins to find the total value	49	3.11
10	10.3	1.5.B	May not understand that the final number counted is the total number of shoes	54	31.04
11	10.7	1.5.C	May have difficulty counting when the numbers cross 100	58	28.14
12	11.1	1.5.D	May think the problem situation shows subtraction instead of addition	59	10.03

*TEKS—Texas Essential Knowledge and Skills; **RtI**—Response to Intervention

Item	Lesson	TEKS*	Common Error	Intervene with RtI* Tier 1 Lessons	Soar to Success Math
13	11.4	1.5.D	May not be able to make the transition from word problem to number sentence	62	29.33
14	13.6	1.5.E	May think the missing number is the difference for 11 − 2	63	29.29, 29.30
15	13.4	1.5.F	May not understand that the same number is the unknown in both related sentences	71	29.21
16	13.2	1.5.F	May subtract 9 and 9 instead of adding them	69	29.31
17	15.2	1.6.B	May mistakenly think that size and color are features that define a shape	75	39.17, 39.26
18	14.2	1.6.D	May confuse a hexagon with a pentagon	74	38.12
19	15.3	1.6.E	May not know the meaning of "face," "edge," and "vertices"	76	39.13, 39.19
20	16.2	1.6.G	May think halves show three equal parts	83	5.03
21	16.3	1.6.H	May not be able to visualize whether the parts are equal	84	5.05
22	17.1	1.7.A	May not understand the concept of comparing lengths	85	41.05
23	18.2	1.7.E	May think the clock shows time to the hour	90	51.10
24	19.1	1.8.C	May forget to subtract when comparing two numbers	97	54.04
25	20.3	1.9.C	May add the two numbers instead of counting by fives	43	29.29, 29.30

*TEKS—Texas Essential Knowledge and Skills; RtI—Response to Intervention

Child's Name _____ Date _____

Beginning of the Year Test

Item	Lesson	TEKS*	Common Error	Intervene with RtI* Tier 1 Lessons	Soar to Success Math
1	1.6	2.2.B	May not understand that a number can be written in different ways	9	2.21
2	3.5	2.2.D	May not know how to use the < and > symbols	11	7.26
3	2.4	2.2.E	May not know how to identify a whole number on an open number line	16	35.14
4	2.2	2.2.D	May not know how to use comparative language	12	7.23, 7.25
5	2.4	2.2.F	May not know how to identify the whole number that corresponds to a specific point on a number line	16	35.14
6	4.1	2.3.A	May not be able to identify halves of a whole	17	5.04
7	4.2	2.3.B	May not understand that the more fractional parts used to make a whole, the smaller the parts are	18	5.04
8	4.4	2.3.C	May not know how to count fractional parts using words	20	5.07
9	4.4	2.3.D	May not know how to recognize examples and non-examples of eighths	20	5.07
10	5.1	2.4.A	May not understand how to use doubles facts to add	22	10.14
11	6.1	2.4.B	May not regroup 10 ones as 1 ten	28	10.29
12	9.4	2.4.C	May not complete all parts of the problem	43	14.18
13	9.5	2.4.D	May not understand how to write a number sentence to represent the problem	51	10.36, 11.26
14	11.1	2.5.A	May not include the value of the dimes	53	3.10, 3.11

*TEKS—Texas Essential Knowledge and Skills; RtI—Response to Intervention

Child's Name _____ Date _____

Beginning of the Year Test (continued)

Item	Lesson	TEKS*	Common Error	Intervene with RtI* Tier 1 Lessons	Soar to Success Math
15	11.3	2.5.A	May not count coins in order of value	55	3.11, 3.12
16	12.1	2.6.A	May not understand how to use the model to solve the problem	57	12.18
17	12.4	2.6.B	May not understand how to interpret representations for separating objects into equivalent sets	60	13.08
18	13.1	2.7.A	May not know how to identify an even or odd number	63	27.11
19	13.2	2.7.B	May not understand how to identify a number that is 10 more or 10 less than a given number	64	28.14
20	13.4	2.7.C	May not recognize the situation as calling for addition	66	70.02
21	14.4	2.8.A	May miscount the number of vertices of a two-dimensional shape	68	38.18
22	15.1	2.8.B	May not be able to classify three-dimensional solids based on attributes	69	39.26
23	14.2	2.8.C	May not know how to identify the number of sides of a two-dimensional shape	72	38.15
24	14.3	2.8.D	May miscount the sides a two-dimensional shape composed of other two-dimensional shapes has	74	38.17
25	14.5	2.8.E	May not understand how to take apart a two-dimensional shape to make a new two-dimensional shape	76	38.19
26	16.3	2.9.B	May not know the relationship between an inch and a foot	78	41.06
27	16.1	2.9.A	May add incorrectly when determining the solution to a problem involving length	77	41.07

*TEKS—Texas Essential Knowledge and Skills; **RtI**—Response to Intervention

Beginning of the Year Test (continued)

Item	Lesson	TEKS*	Common Error	Intervene with RtI* Tier 1 Lessons	Soar to Success Math
28	17.2	2.9.C	May not know how to use the diagram to find the length	80	35.14
29	16.5	2.9.D	May have difficulty estimating the length of an object	81	41.16
30	16.4	2.9.E	May not know the relationship between an inch and a foot	84	41.10
31	17.4	2.9.F	May not understand how to use square units to find the area of a rectangle	85	48.15
32	18.1	2.9.G	May not read time correctly to the nearest minute	86	51.08, 51.10
33	19.6	2.10.B	May not understand how to use pictures to complete a row of a pictograph	94	54.23
34	19.5	2.10.C	May not understand how to use a bar graph to solve an addition problem	95	54.16
35	19.7	2.10.D	May not correctly draw conclusions from the data in a bar graph	96	54.15
36	20.2	2.11.A	May not correctly calculate how many weeks it will take to save an amount of money	57	12.18
37	20.3	2.11.C	May not understand that a deposit involves addition and a withdrawal involves subtraction	32	10.34
38	20.4	2.11.D	May not correctly calculate the amount of money to borrow for a given purchase	38	11.23, 11.24
39	20.5	2.11.E	May not know how to calculate how long it will take to pay back a loan	39	11.23, 11.24
40	20.6	2.11.F	May not understand the problem is a multi-step problem	32	10.34

*TEKS—Texas Essential Knowledge and Skills; RtI—Response to Intervention

Child's Name _____ Date _____

Middle of the Year Test

Item	Lesson	TEKS*	Common Error	Intervene with RtI* Tier 1 Lessons	Soar to Success Math
1	1.6	2.2.B	May not understand that a number can be written in different ways	9	2.21
2	3.4	2.2.C	May not know to use the < and the > symbols	14	7.24
3	2.3	2.2.D	May not know how to use comparative language	13	7.19
4	2.4	2.2.E	May not know how to identify a whole number that corresponds to a specific point on a number line	16	35.14
5	2.4	2.2.F	May not know how to identify a whole number that corresponds to a specific point on a number line	16	35.14
6	4.1	2.3.A	May not be able to identify halves of a whole	17	5.04
7	4.2	2.3.B	May not understand that the more fractional parts used to make a whole, the smaller the parts are	18	5.04
8	4.3	2.3.C	May not know how to count fractional parts using words	19	5.04
9	4.4	2.3.D	May not know how to recognize eighths as equal parts of a whole	20	5.07
10	5.3	2.4.A	May not understand how addition facts are related to subtraction facts	24	11.15
11	6.3	2.4.B	May not regroup 10 ones as 1 ten	29	10.30
12	9.4	2.4.C	May not complete all the steps in the problem	43	14.18
13	9.5	2.4.D	May not recognize the situation as calling for addition	51	10.36, 11.26
14	11.2	2.5.A	May not include the value of a nickel	54	3.13

*TEKS—Texas Essential Knowledge and Skills; **RtI**—Response to Intervention

Child's Name _____ Date _____

Middle of the Year Test (continued)

Item	Lesson	TEKS*	Common Error	Intervene with RtI* Tier 1 Lessons	Soar to Success Math
15	11.4	2.5.B	May not understand how to read symbols for money	56	3.11, 3.12
16	12.3	2.6.A	May not recognize the model as equal sets being joined together	59	12.19
17	12.6	2.6.B	May not understand how to interpret representations for separating objects into equivalent sets	62	13.08
18	13.1	2.7.A	May not correctly identify an even or odd number	63	27.11
19	13.2	2.7.B	May not understand how to identify numbers that are 10 more or 10 less than a given number	64	28.14
20	13.5	2.7.C	May not recognize the addition sentence as a way to represent the problem	67	14.18
21	14.4	2.8.A	May miscount the number of vertices a two-dimensional shape has	68	38.18
22	15.2	2.8.B	May not be able to classify three-dimensional solids based on attributes	70	39.33
23	14.6	2.8.C	May not know how to identify the number of sides a two-dimensional shape has	73	38.11
24	15.3	2.8.D	May miscount units in a rectangular prism composed of unit cubes	75	39.29
25	14.5	2.8.E	May not understand how to take apart a two-dimensional shape to make a new two-dimensional shape	76	38.19
26	16.3	2.9.B	May not understand the relationship of inches to feet	78	41.06
27	16.1	2.9.A	May not understand the relationship of inches to feet	77	41.07

*TEKS—Texas Essential Knowledge and Skills; **RtI**—Response to Intervention

© Houghton Mifflin Harcourt Publishing Company

Child's Name _____ Date _____

Middle of the Year Test (continued)

Item	Lesson	TEKS*	Common Error	Intervene with RtI* Tier 1 Lessons	Soar to Success Math
28	17.2	2.9.C	May not know how to use the diagram to find the length	80	35.14
29	16.5	2.9.D	May have difficulty estimating the length of an object	81	41.16
30	16.4	2.9.E	May not know the relationship between an inch and a foot	84	41.10
31	17.4	2.9.F	May not understand how to use square units to find the area of a rectangle	85	48.15
32	18.2	2.9.G	May not read time correctly to the nearest minute	87	51.11
33	19.6	2.10.B	May not understand how to use the numbers to complete a row of a bar graph	94	54.23
34	19.5	2.10.C	May not draw correct conclusions from a pictograph	95	54.16
35	19.7	2.10.D	May not understand how to use data in a bar graph to make predictions	96	54.15
36	20.2	2.11.A	May not know how to correctly calculate how long it will take to save an amount of money	57	12.18
37	20.3	2.11.C	May not understand that a deposit involves addition and a withdrawal involves subtraction	32	10.34
38	20.4	2.11.D	May not correctly calculate the amount of money to borrow for a given purchase	38	11.23, 11.24
39	20.5	2.11.E	May not know how to calculate how long it will take to pay back a loan	39	11.23, 11.24
40	20.6	2.11.F	May not know the difference between a producer and a consumer	32	10.34

*TEKS—Texas Essential Knowledge and Skills; RtI—Response to Intervention

Child's Name _____ Date _____

End of the Year Test

Item	Lesson	TEKS*	Common Error	Intervene with RtI* Tier 1 Lessons	Soar to Success Math
1	1.5	2.2.B	May not understand that a number can be written in different ways	3	1.20
2	3.5	2.2.D	May not know to use comparative language	11	7.26
3	2.2	2.2.D	May not know how to use the < and > symbols	12	7.23, 7.25
4	2.4	2.2.E	May not know how to identify a whole number on an open number line	16	35.14
5	2.4	2.2.F	May not know how to identify the whole number that corresponds to a specific point on a number line	16	35.14
6	4.1	2.3.A	May not be able to identify eighths of a whole	17	5.04
7	4.2	2.3.B	May not understand that the more fractional parts used to make a whole, the smaller the parts are	18	5.04
8	4.4	2.3.C	May not know how to count fractional parts using words	20	5.07
9	4.4	2.3.D	May not know how to recognize examples and non examples of halves	20	5.07
10	5.5	2.4.A	May not understand how to use doubles facts to add	26	11.17
11	7.4	2.4.B	May not regroup 10 ones as 1 ten	33	10.37
12	9.4	2.4.C	May not recognize the situation as a two-part problem	43	14.18
13	9.5	2.4.D	May not recognize the situation as calling for addition	51	10.36, 11.26
14	11.1	2.5.A	May not include the value of a nickel	53	3.10, 3.11

*TEKS—Texas Essential Knowledge and Skills; RtI—Response to Intervention

© Houghton Mifflin Harcourt Publishing Company

Child's Name _____ Date _____

End of the Year Test (continued)

Item	Lesson	TEKS*	Common Error	Intervene with RtI* Tier 1 Lessons	Soar to Success Math
15	11.3	2.5.B	May not understand how to use money symbols to write an amount of money	55	3.11, 3.12
16	12.2	2.6.A	May not understand the concept of combining equal sets	58	12.19
17	12.5	2.6.B	May not understand how to interpret contextual situations for separating objects into equivalent sets	61	13.08
18	13.1	2.7.A	May not know how to identify an even or odd number	63	27.11
19	13.3	2.7.B	May not understand the meaning of 100 fewer	65	10.38
20	13.5	2.7.C	May not be able to match a number sentence to a situation	67	14.18
21	14.4	2.8.A	May miscount the number of vertices a two-dimensional shape has	68	38.18
22	15.2	2.8.B	May not be able to classify three-dimensional solids based on attributes	70	39.33
23	14.6	2.8.C	May not know how to identify the number of sides a two-dimensional shape has	73	38.11
24	15.3	2.8.D	May miscount units in a rectangular prism composed of unit cubes	75	39.29
25	14.5	2.8.E	May not understand how to take apart a two-dimensional shape to make a new two-dimensional shape	76	38.19
26	16.3	2.9.B	May not know the relationship between an inch and a foot	78	41.06
27	16.1	2.9.A	May not know the relationship between an inch and a foot	77	41.07

*TEKS—Texas Essential Knowledge and Skills; **RtI**—Response to Intervention

End of the Year Test (continued)

Item	Lesson	TEKS*	Common Error	Intervene with RtI* Tier 1 Lessons	Soar to Success Math
28	17.2	2.9.C	May not understand how to use the diagram to find the length	80	35.14
29	16.5	2.9.D	May have difficulty estimating the length of an object	81	41.16
30	16.4	2.9.E	May not know the relationship between an inch and a foot to make a prediction of length	84	41.10
31	17.4	2.9.F	May not understand how to use square units to find the area of a rectangle	85	48.15
32	18.4	2.9.G	May not understand A.M. and P.M.	88	51.15
33	19.6	2.10.B	May not understand how to use bars to complete a bar graph	94	54.23
34	19.5	2.10.C	May not understand how to interpret a bar graph	95	54.16
35	19.7	2.10.D	May not draw correct conclusions from a bar graph	96	54.15
36	20.2	2.11.A	May not know how to correctly calculate how long it will take to save an amount of money	57	12.18
37	20.3	2.11.C	May not understand that a deposit involves addition and a withdrawal involves subtraction	32	10.34
38	20.4	2.11.D	May not correctly calculate the amount of money to borrow for a given purchase	38	11.23, 11.24
39	20.5	2.11.E	May not know how to calculate how long it will take to pay back a loan	39	11.23, 11.24
40	20.6	2.11.F	May not know the difference between a producer and a consumer	32	10.34

*TEKS—Texas Essential Knowledge and Skills; RtI—Response to Intervention

Child's Name _____ Date _____

Module 1 Test

Item	Lesson	TEKS*	Common Error	Intervene with RtI* Tier 1 Lessons	Soar to Success
1	1.1	2.2.B	May not know how to identify a number in word form	8	2.17
2	1.6	2.2.B	May not understand that a number can be written in different ways	9	2.21
3	1.1	2.2.B	May not understand that a number can be written in different ways	1	2.20
4	1.2	2.2.E	May not understand how to locate the position of a number on a number line	15	15.13
5	1.3	2.2.A	May not recognize a number being modeled	1	2.20
6	1.4	2.2.A	May not correctly identify the place value of digits	2	1.20
7	1.5	2.2.A	May not correctly identify the place value of digits	3	1.20
8	1.7	2.2.A	May not recognize a number in expanded form	4	1.23
9	1.2	2.2.F	May not understand how to locate the position of a number on a number line	15	15.13
10	1.7	2.2.A	May miscount blocks representing thousands, hundreds, tens, or ones	4	1.23
11	1.2	2.2.E	May not understand how to locate the position of a number on a number line	15	15.13
12	1.4	2.2.A	May not correctly identify the place value of digits	2	1.20

***TEKS**—Texas Essential Knowledge and Skills; **RtI**—Response to Intervention

Child's Name _____ Date _____

Module 2 Test

Item	Lesson	TEKS*	Common Error	Intervene with RtI* Tier 1 Lessons	Soar to Success
1	2.1	2.2.A	May miscount quick pictures of place value blocks	5	2.23
2	2.1	2.2.A	May not recognize a number in expanded form	5	2.23
3	2.1	2.2.B	May not correctly identify the place value of the digits	5	2.23
4	2.1	2.2.B	May not correctly identify the place value of the digits	5	2.23
5	2.2	2.2.D	May not know how to use comparative language	12	7.23, 7.25
6	2.2	2.2.D	May not know how to use the $<$, $>$, and $=$ symbols	12	7.23, 7.25
7	2.3	2.2.D	May not know how to use the $<$, $>$, and $=$ symbols	13	7.19
8	2.3	2.2.D	May not know how to use the $<$, $>$, and $=$ symbols	13	7.19
9	2.4	2.2.E	May not know how to locate the position of a whole number on an open number line	16	35.14
10	2.4	2.2.E	May not know how to locate the position of a whole number on an open number line	16	35.14
11	2.4	2.2.F	May not know how to name the whole number that corresponds to a specific point on a number line	16	35.14
12	2.4	2.2.F	May not know how to name the whole number that corresponds to a specific point on a number line	16	35.14

*TEKS—Texas Essential Knowledge and Skills; RtI—Response to Intervention

Child's Name _____ Date _____

Module 3 Test

Item	Lesson	TEKS*	Common Error	Intervene with RtI* Tier 1 Lessons	Soar to Success
1	3.1	2.2.A	May miscount base-ten blocks	6	2.16
2	3.1	2.2.A	May miscount base-ten blocks	6	2.16
3	3.1	2.2.A	May miscount quick pictures of base-ten blocks	6	2.16
4	3.2	2.2.B	May not correctly identify the place value of the digits	10	2.23
5	3.2	2.2.B	May not understand how to write a number in expanded form	10	2.23
6	3.2	2.2.B	May not understand how to write a number in expanded form	10	2.23
7	3.5	2.2.D	May not know how to use comparative language	11	7.26
8	3.5	2.2.D	May not know how to use the $<$, $>$, and $=$ symbols	11	7.26
9	3.5	2.2.D	May not know how to use the $<$, $>$, and $=$ symbols	11	7.26
10	3.5	2.2.D	May confuse digits in the thousands, hundreds, tens, and ones places	11	7.26
11	3.5	2.2.D	May not know how to use comparative language	11	7.26
12	3.5	2.2.D	May not know how to use comparative language	11	7.26

*TEKS—Texas Essential Knowledge and Skills; **RtI**—Response to Intervention

Child's Name _____ Date _____

Module 4 Test

Item	Lesson	TEKS*	Common Error	Intervene with RtI* Tier 1 Lessons	Soar to Success
1	4.1	2.3.A	May not be able to identify halves of a whole	17	5.04
2	4.2	2.3.B	May not understand the more fractional parts used to make a whole, the smaller the part	18	5.04
3	4.3	2.3.B	May not understand that the fewer the fractional parts, the larger the part	19	5.04
4	4.3	2.3.B	May not understand the more fractional parts used to make a whole, the smaller the part	19	5.04
5	4.3	2.3.B	May not understand that the fewer the fractional parts, the larger the part	19	5.04
6	4.3	2.3.B	May not understand that the more fractional parts used to make a whole, the smaller the part	19	5.04
7	4.4	2.3.C	May not know how to count fractional parts using words	20	5.07
8	4.4	2.3.D	May not know how to recognize how many parts it takes to equal one whole	20	5.07
9	4.4	2.3.D	May not be able to identify examples and non-examples of halves, fourths, and eighths	20	5.07
10	4.5	2.3.C	May not understand how to identify fractional parts beyond one whole using words	21	5.07
11	4.5	2.3.C	May not understand how to identify fractional parts beyond one whole using words	21	5.07
12	4.5	2.3.C	May not understand how to identify fractional parts beyond one whole using words	21	5.07

*TEKS—Texas Essential Knowledge and Skills; **RtI**—Response to Intervention

Module 5 Test

Item	Lesson	TEKS*	Common Error	Intervene with RtI* Tier 1 Lessons	Soar to Success Math
1	5.1	2.4.A	May not understand how to use doubles facts to add	22	10.14
2	5.1	2.4.A	May not understand how to use doubles facts to add	22	10.14
3	5.2	2.4.A	May not understand how to make a ten to add	23	10.20
4	5.2	2.4.A	May not understand how to make a ten to add	23	10.20
5	5.3	2.4.A	May not understand how to use related addition facts to subtract	24	10.21, 11.15
6	5.3	2.4.A	May use an incorrect operation to solve	24	10.21, 11.15
7	5.4	2.4.A	May not understand how to use tens facts to subtract	25	10.29
8	5.4	2.4.A	May not understand how to use tens facts to subtract	25	10.29
9	5.5	2.4.C	May not understand how to make a ten to add	26	11.17
10	5.5	2.4.C	May not understand how to make a ten to add	26	11.17
11	5.5	2.4.C	May use an incorrect operation to solve	26	11.17
12	5.5	2.4.C	May use an incorrect operation to solve	26	11.17

*TEKS—Texas Essential Knowledge and Skills; RtI—Response to Intervention

Child's Name _____ Date _____

Module 6 Test

Item	Lesson	TEKS*	Common Error	Intervene with RtI* Tier 1 Lessons	Soar to Success Math
1	6.1	2.4.B	May not regroup 10 ones as 1 ten	27	10.20
2	6.1	2.4.B	May add incorrectly	27	10.20
3	6.1	2.4.B	May not regroup	27	10.20
4	6.2	2.4.B	May not regroup 10 ones as 1 ten	28	10.29
5	6.2	2.4.B	May not understand how to make an addend a 10 to solve an addition problem	28	10.29
6	6.2	2.4.B	May not understand how to make an addend a 10 to solve an addition problem	28	10.29
7	6.3	2.4.B	May not understand how to break apart addends to add tens and then add ones	29	10.30
8	6.3	2.4.B	May not understand how to break apart addends to add tens and then add ones	29	10.30
9	6.3	2.4.B	May not understand how to break apart addends to add tens and then add ones	29	10.30
10	6.4	2.4.B	May not regroup	30	10.34
11	6.4	2.4.B	May not know when to regroup	30	10.34
12	6.4	2.4.B	May not regroup	30	10.34

*TEKS—Texas Essential Knowledge and Skills; **RtI**—Response to Intervention

Child's Name _____ Date _____

Module 7 Test

Item	Lesson	TEKS*	Common Error	Intervene with RtI* Tier 1 Lessons	Soar to Success Math
1	7.1	2.4.B	May not understand when to regroup	31	10.34
2	7.1	2.4.B	May subtract instead of adding in the second step of the problem	31	10.34
3	7.2	2.4.B	May add incorrectly	32	10.34
4	7.2	2.4.B	May not understand when to regroup	32	10.34
5	7.4	2.4.B	May not add the third addend	33	10.37
6	7.4	2.4.B	May not add the third addend	33	10.37
7	7.5	2.4.B	May not add the fourth addend	34	10.37
8	7.5	2.4.B	May not add the fourth addend	34	10.37
9	7.3	2.4.C	May not understand how to write a number sentence to represent the problem	40	10.36
10	7.3	2.4.C	May not understand how to write a number sentence to represent the problem	40	10.36
11	7.3	2.4.C	May not understand how to write a number sentence to represent the problem	40	10.36
12	7.3	2.4.C	May not understand how to write a number sentence to represent the problem	40	10.36

*TEKS—Texas Essential Knowledge and Skills; RtI—Response to Intervention

Child's Name _____ Date _____

Unit 1 Test

Item	Lesson	TEKS*	Common Error	Intervene with RtI* Tier 1 Lessons	Soar to Success Math
1	1.4	2.2.A	May not correctly identify the place value of digits	2	1.20
2	3.3	2.2.A	May miscount blocks representing hundreds, tens, and ones.	7	2.23
3	1.7	2.2.A	May miscount blocks representing hundreds, tens, and ones	4	1.23
4	2.1	2.2.B	May not understand that a number can be written in different ways	5	2.23
5	3.2	2.2.B	May not correctly identify the place value of the digits	10	2.23
6	3.4	2.2.C	May not understand how to find the missing quantity	14	7.24
7	3.4	2.2.C	May not know how to use the <, >, and = symbols	14	7.24
8	2.2	2.2.D	May not know how to use comparative language	12	7.23, 7.25
9	3.5	2.2.D	May not know how to use the <, >, and = symbols	11	7.26
10	2.3	2.2.D	May not know how to use the <, >, and = symbols	13	7.19
11	4.1	2.3.A	May not be able to identify fourths of a whole	17	5.04
12	4.2	2.3.B	May not understand that the more fractional parts used to make a whole, the smaller the parts are	18	5.04

*TEKS—Texas Essential Knowledge and Skills; **RtI**—Response to Intervention

Unit 1 Test (continued)

Item	Lesson	TEKS*	Common Error	Intervene with RtI* Tier 1 Lessons	Soar to Success Math
13	4.2	2.3.B	May not understand that the that the fewer the fractional parts, the larger the parts are	18	5.04
14	4.5	2.3.C	May not understand how to identify fractional parts beyond one whole using words	21	5.07
15	4.4	2.3.C	May not understand how to identify fractional parts beyond one whole using words	20	5.07
16	5.5	2.4.C	May not understand how to make a ten to add	26	11.17
17	6.1	2.4.B	May not regroup	27	10.20
18	7.5	2.4.B	May not add the fourth addend	34	10.37

*TEKS—Texas Essential Knowledge and Skills; **RtI**—Response to Intervention

Module 8 Test

Item	Lesson	TEKS*	Common Error	Intervene with RtI* Tier 1 Lessons	Soar to Success Math
1	8.1	2.4.B	May not regroup 10 ones as 1 ten	35	11.19
2	8.1	2.4.B	May subtract incorrectly	35	11.19
3	8.1	2.4.B	May subtract incorrectly	35	11.19
4	8.2	2.4.B	May not understand how to use the number line correctly	36	11.22
5	8.2	2.4.B	May not understand when to regroup	36	11.22
6	8.2	2.4.B	May not use the correct operation to solve	36	11.22
7	8.3	2.4.B	May add instead of subtract	37	11.24
8	8.3	2.4.B	May forget to complete all the steps to solve the problem	37	11.24
9	8.3	2.4.B	May not reduce the number in the tens column after regrouping	37	11.24
10	8.4	2.4.C	May subtract incorrectly	41	11.23,11.24
11	8.4	2.4.C	May not understand when to regroup	41	11.23,11.24
12	8.4	2.4.C	May subtract incorrectly	41	11.23,11.24

*TEKS—Texas Essential Knowledge and Skills; RtI—Response to Intervention

Child's Name _____ Date _____

Module 9 Test

Item	Lesson	TEKS*	Common Error	Intervene with RtI* Tier 1 Lessons	Soar to Success Math
1	9.1	2.4.B	May add instead of subtracting	38	11.23, 11.24
2	9.2	2.4.B	May add instead of subtract	39	11.23, 11.24
3	9.2	2.4.C	May add instead of subtract	39	11.23, 11.24
4	9.3	2.4.C	May not understand how to write a number sentence to represent the problem	42	11.26
5	9.4	2.3.C	May not understand how to write a number sentence to represent the problem	43	14.18
6	9.4	2.4.C	May add the wrong numbers	43	14.18
7	9.4	2.4.C	May subtract the numbers given in the problem	43	14.18
8	9.4	2.4.C	May omit a step needed to solve the problem	43	14.18
9	9.4	2.4.C	May subtract any two numbers given in the problem	43	14.18
10	9.4	2.4.C	May omit a step needed to solve the problem	43	14.18
11	9.5	2.4.D	May not understand how to write a number sentence to represent the problem	51	10.36, 11.26
12	9.5	2.4.D	May not understand how to write a number sentence to represent the problem	51	10.36, 11.26

*TEKS—Texas Essential Knowledge and Skills; **RtI**—Response to Intervention

Module 10 Test

Item	Lesson	TEKS*	Common Error	Intervene with RtI* Tier 1 Lessons	Soar to Success Math
1	10.1	2.4.C	May not regroup 10 ones for a ten	44	10.30
2	10.2	2.4.C	May not regroup 10 ones for a ten	45	10.40, 10.41
3	10.3	2.4.C	May not regroup 10 ones for a ten	46	10.40, 10.41
4	10.4	2.4.C	May add instead of subtracting to solve the problem	47	11.28
5	10.5	2.4.C	May incorrectly subtract the tens	48	11.29
6	10.6	2.4.C	May not regroup one hundred as tens to subtract	49	11.30
7	10.7	2.4.C	May omit a step to solve the problem	50	11.17
8	10.7	2.4.C	May add instead of subtracting	50	11.17
9	10.7	2.4.C	May omit a step to solve the problem	50	11.17
10	10.8	2.4.D	May not understand how to write a number sentence to represent the problem	52	11.17
11	10.8	2.4.D	May not understand how to write a number sentence to represent the problem	52	11.17
12	10.8	2.4.D	May not understand how to write a number sentence to represent the problem	52	11.17

*TEKS—Texas Essential Knowledge and Skills; **RtI**—Response to Intervention

Child's Name _____ Date _____

Module 11 Test

Item	Lesson	TEKS*	Common Error	Intervene with RtI* Tier 1 Lessons	Soar to Success Math
1	11.1	2.5.B	May not include the value of a nickel	53	3.10, 3.11
2	11.1	2.5.B	May not include the value of all the nickels	53	3.10, 3.11
3	11.1	2.5.B	May only count the value of one dime	53	3.10, 3.11
4	11.3	2.5.B	May not count coins in order of value	55	3.11, 3.12
5	11.3	2.5.B	May not include the value of one of the dimes	55	3.11, 3.12
6	11.3	2.5.B	May not include the value of the dime	55	3.11, 3.12
7	11.2	2.5.B	May not understand how to use the dollar sign and the decimal point to show the value of a dollar	54	3.13
8	11.2	2.5.B	May not understand how to use the dollar sign and the decimal point to name the value of a collection of coins	54	3.13
9	11.2	2.5.B	May confuse the dollar and cents signs	54	3.13
10	11.4	2.5.B	May confuse the value of a dime and a nickel	56	3.11, 3.12
11	11.4	2.5.B	May incorrectly count the value of the coins	56	3.11, 3.12
12	11.4	2.5.B	May not count the value of the dimes	56	3.11, 3.12

*TEKS—Texas Essential Knowledge and Skills; RtI—Response to Intervention

Child's Name _____ Date _____

Module 12 Test

Item	Lesson	TEKS*	Common Error	Intervene with RtI* Tier 1 Lessons	Soar to Success Math
1	12.1	2.6.A	May add the number of bags and the number of toys in a bag	57	12.18
2	12.3	2.6.A	May not understand how to interpret representations of equal groups	59	12.19
3	12.3	2.6.A	May not understand how to interpret representations of equal groups	59	12.19
4	12.3	2.6.A	May not understand how to interpret representations of equal groups	59	12.19
5	12.2	2.6.A	May not understand how to interpret multiplication situations for joining equivalent sets	58	12.19
6	12.4	2.6.B	May not understand how to interpret representations for separating objects into equivalent sets	60	13.08
7	12.4	2.6.B	May not understand how to interpret division situations for separating objects into equivalent sets	60	13.08
8	12.6	2.6.B	May not understand how to interpret division situations for separating objects into equivalent sets	62	13.08
9	12.6	2.6.B	May not understand how to interpret division situations for separating objects into equivalent sets	62	13.08
10	12.5	2.6.B	May not understand how to describe division situations for separating objects into equivalent sets	61	13.08
11	12.5	2.6.B	May not understand how to describe division situations for separating objects into equivalent sets	61	13.08
12	12.5	2.6.B	May not understand how to describe division situations for separating objects into equivalent sets	61	13.08

*TEKS—Texas Essential Knowledge and Skills; RtI—Response to Intervention

Child's Name _____ Date _____

Unit 2 Test

Item	Lesson	TEKS*	Common Error	Intervene with RtI* Tier 1 Lessons	Soar to Success Math
1	8.1	2.4.B	May subtract incorrectly	35	11.19
2	10.3	2.4.C	May add incorrectly	46	10.40, 10.41
3	9.4	2.4.C	May add instead of subtracting	43	14.18
4	9.4	2.4.C	May omit a step needed to solve the problem	43	14.18
5	10.7	2.4.C	May omit a step needed to solve the problem	50	11.17
6	10.8	2.4.D	May not understand how to write a number sentence to represent a problem	52	11.17
7	11.1	2.5.B	May incorrectly count the value of a nickel as ten cents	53	3.10, 3.11
8	11.3	2.5.B	May confuse nickels and dimes	55	3.10, 3.11
9	11.2	2.5.B	May not understand how to use the dollar sign and decimal point to name the value of a dollar	54	3.13
10	11.4	2.5.B	May not subtract the amount of money spent	56	3.11, 3.12

*TEKS—Texas Essential Knowledge and Skills; **RtI**—Response to Intervention

© Houghton Mifflin Harcourt Publishing Company

Unit 2 Test (continued)

Item	Lesson	TEKS*	Common Error	Intervene with RtI* Tier 1 Lessons	Soar to Success Math
11	12.1	2.6.A	May not understand how to describe multiplication situations for joining equivalent sets	57	12.18
12	12.3	2.6.A	May not understand how to join equivalent sets	59	12.19
13	12.3	2.6.A	May not understand how to interpret division situations for separating objects into equivalent sets	59	12.19
14	12.2	2.6.A	May not understand how to describe division situations for separating objects into equivalent sets	58	12.19
15	12.4	2.6.B	May add instead of identifying the number of items in each equal set	60	13.08
16	12.6	2.6.B	May add instead of identifying the number of items in each equal set	62	13.08
17	12.5	2.6.B	May not separate into equivalent groups	61	13.08
18	12.5	2.6.B	May not separate into equivalent groups	61	13.08

*TEKS—Texas Essential Knowledge and Skills; RtI—Response to Intervention

Child's Name _____ Date _____

Unit 3 Test

Item	Lesson	TEKS*	Common Error	Intervene with RtI* Tier 1 Lessons	Soar to Success Math
1	13.1	2.7.A	May not know how to correctly identify an even or odd number	63	27.11
2	13.2	2.7.B	May not understand the meaning of 10 less	64	28.14
3	13.2	2.7.B	May not understand the meaning of 10 more	64	28.14
4	13.2	2.7.B	May omit a step when solving a multi-step problem	64	28.14
5	13.2	2.7.B	May not understand the meaning of 10 more	64	28.14
6	13.3	2.7.B	May not understand the meaning of 100 fewer	65	10.38
7	13.3	2.7.B	May find a sum instead of a difference	65	10.38
8	13.3	2.7.B	May find a sum instead of a difference	65	10.38
9	13.3	2.7.B	May find a difference instead of a sum	65	10.38
10	13.4	2.7.C	May find a sum instead of a difference	66	70.02
11	13.4	2.7.C	May find a sum instead of a difference	66	70.02
12	13.4	2.7.C	May not understand how to write a number sentence to represent a problem	66	70.02
13	13.4	2.7.C	May add incorrectly	66	70.02
14	13.4	2.7.C	May add incorrectly	66	70.02

*TEKS—Texas Essential Knowledge and Skills; **RtI**—Response to Intervention

Unit 3 Test (continued)

Item	Lesson	TEKS*	Common Error	Intervene with RtI* Tier 1 Lessons	Soar to Success Math
15	13.5	2.7.C	May find a sum instead of a difference	67	14.18
16	13.5	2.7.C	May subtract incorrectly	67	14.18
17	13.5	2.7.C	May not understand how to write a number sentence to represent a problem	67	14.18
18	13.5	2.7.C	May omit a step when solving a multi-step problem	67	14.18

*TEKS—Texas Essential Knowledge and Skills; **RtI**—Response to Intervention

Child's Name _____ Date _____

Module 14 Test

Item	Lesson	TEKS*	Common Error	Intervene with RtI* Tier 1 Lessons	Soar to Success Math
1	14.4	2.8.A	May miscount the number of vertices of two-dimensional shapes	68	38.18
2	14.4	2.8.A	May miscount the number of sides of two-dimensional shapes	68	38.18
3	14.1	2.8.C	May not know how to identify the number of vertices of a two-dimensional shape.	71	39.12
4	14.2	2.8.C	May not know how to identify the number of sides of a two-dimensional shape	72	38.15
5	14.6	2.8.C	May not understand how to sort two-dimensional shapes by number of sides	73	38.11
6	14.6	2.8.C	May not understand how to sort two-dimensional shapes by number of sides	73	38.11
7	14.6	2.8.C	May not understand how to sort two-dimensional shapes by number of vertices	73	38.11
8	14.3	2.8.D	May not understand how to compose new two-dimensional shapes from other two-dimensional shapes	74	38.17
9	14.3	2.8.D	May miscount vertices in new two-dimensional shapes composed of other two-dimensional shapes	74	38.17
10	14.3	2.8.D	May miscount sides in new two-dimensional shapes composed of other two-dimensional shapes	74	38.17
11	14.5	2.8.E	May not understand how to take apart two-dimensional shapes to make new two-dimensional shapes	76	38.19
12	14.5	2.8.E	May not understand how to take apart two-dimensional shapes to make new two-dimensional shapes	76	38.19

*TEKS—Texas Essential Knowledge and Skills; RtI—Response to Intervention

Child's Name _____ Date _____

Module 15 Test

Item	Lesson	TEKS*	Common Error	Intervene with RtI* Tier 1 Lessons	Soar to Success Math
1	15.1	2.8.B	May not be able to classify three-dimensional solids based on attributes	69	39.26
2	15.1	2.8.B	May not be able to classify three-dimensional solids based on attributes	69	39.26
3	15.1	2.8.B	May not be able to classify three-dimensional solids based on attributes	69	39.26
4	15.2	2.8.B	May not be able to sort three-dimensional solids based on attributes	70	39.33
5	15.2	2.8.B	May not be able to sort three-dimensional solids based on attributes	70	39.33
6	15.2	2.8.B	May not be able to sort three-dimensional solids based on attributes	70	39.33
7	15.2	2.8.B	May miscount vertices of a three-dimensional solid	70	39.33
8	15.3	2.8.D	May not understand how to compose three-dimensional solids based on given attributes	75	39.29
9	15.3	2.8.D	May not understand how to compose three-dimensional solids based on given attributes	75	39.29
10	15.3	2.8.D	May not correctly identify the number of unit cubes used to compose a three-dimensional solids	75	39.29
11	15.3	2.8.D	May not correctly identify the number of unit cubes used to compose a three-dimensional solid	75	39.29
12	15.3	2.8.D	May not correctly identify the number of unit cubes used to compose a three-dimensional solid	75	39.29

*TEKS—Texas Essential Knowledge and Skills; **RtI**—Response to Intervention

Child's Name _____ Date _____

Module 16 Test

Item	Lesson	TEKS*	Common Error	Intervene with RtI* Tier 1 Lessons	Soar to Success Math
1	16.1	2.9.A	May think the total number of tiles shown indicates the length of the object	77	41.07
2	16.1	2.9.A	May add incorrectly when determining the solution to a problem involving length	77	41.07
3	16.3	2.9.B	May not know the relationship between an inch and a foot	78	41.06
4	16.3	2.9.B	May not know the relationship between an inch and a foot	78	41.06
5	16.2	2.9.D	May not line up the zero mark of the ruler with the edge of the object when measuring	83	41.10
6	16.5	2.9.D	May have difficulty estimating the length of an object	81	41.16
7	16.4	2.9.E	May estimate incorrectly when determining the solution to a problem involving length	84	41.10
8	16.4	2.9.E	May not know the relationship between an inch and a foot	84	41.10
9	16.4	2.9.E	May use an incorrect operation when determining the solution to a problem involving length	84	41.10
10	16.4	2.9.E	May not know the relationship between an inch and a foot	84	41.10
11	16.4	2.9.E	May not know the relationship between an inch and a foot	84	41.10
12	16.4	2.9.E	May have difficulty estimating the length of an object	84	41.10

*TEKS—Texas Essential Knowledge and Skills; RtI—Response to Intervention

Child's Name _____ Date _____

Module 17 Test

Item	Lesson	TEKS*	Common Error	Intervene with RtI* Tier 1 Lessons	Soar to Success Math
1	17.2	2.9.C	May not know how to use the diagram to find the length	80	
2	17.2	2.9.C	May not know how to use the diagram to find the length	80	
3	17.2	2.9.C	May not know how to use the diagram to find the length	80	
4	17.2	2.9.C	May subtract incorrectly	80	
5	17.1	2.9.D	May not line up the zero mark of the ruler with the edge of the object when measuring	82	41.14
6	17.1	2.9.D	May not line up the zero mark of the ruler with the edge of the object when measuring	82	41.14
7	17.3	2.9.D	May not recognize a reasonable measure for a given object	79	41.13
8	17.3	2.9.D	May not line up the zero mark of the ruler with the edge of the object when measuring	79	41.13
9	17.4	2.9.F	May not understand how to use square units to find the area of a rectangle	85	
10	17.4	2.9.F	May not understand how to use square units to find the area of a rectangle	85	
11	17.4	2.9.F	May not understand how to use square units to find the area of a rectangle	85	
12	17.4	2.9.F	May not complete all the steps to solve the problem	85	

*TEKS—Texas Essential Knowledge and Skills; RtI—Response to Intervention

Child's Name _____ Date _____

Module 18 Test

Item	Lesson	TEKS*	Common Error	Intervene with RtI* Tier 1 Lessons	Soar to Success Math
1	18.1	2.9.G	May not correctly read the time to the nearest minute	86	51.08, 51.10
2	18.1	2.9.G	May confuse the minute and hour hand	86	51.08, 51.10
3	18.2	2.9.G	May not correctly read the time to the nearest minute	87	51.11
4	18.2	2.9.G	May confuse the minute and hour hand	87	51.11
5	18.3	2.9.G	May not correctly read the time to the nearest minute	88	51.13
6	18.3	2.9.G	May not correctly read the time to the nearest minute	88	51.13
7	18.4	2.9.G	May not understand A.M. and P.M.	89	51.15
8	18.4	2.9.G	May not understand A.M. and P.M.	89	51.15
9	18.4	2.9.G	May not understand A.M. and P.M.	89	51.15
10	18.4	2.9.G	May not correctly read the time to the nearest minute	89	51.15
11	18.4	2.9.G	May not understand A.M. and P.M.	89	51.15
12	18.4	2.9.G	May not correctly read the time to the nearest minute	89	51.15

*TEKS—Texas Essential Knowledge and Skills; **RtI**—Response to Intervention

Unit 4 Test

Item	Lesson	TEKS*	Common Error	Intervene with RtI* Tier 1 Lessons	Soar to Success Math
1	15.1	2.8.B	May not be able to identify a real-world object that matches a given three-dimensional shape	69	39.26
2	15.2	2.8.B	May not be able to identify three-dimensional solids based on attributes	70	
3	14.1	2.8.C	May not know how to identify the number of vertices a two-dimensional shape has	71	39.12
4	14.6	2.8.C	May not know how to identify the number of sides of a two dimensional shape	73	
5	14.6	2.8.C	May not understand how to sort two-dimensional shapes by number of vertices	73	
6	14.3	2.8.D	May miscount vertices in new two-dimensional shapes composed of other two-dimensional shapes	74	
7	14.3	2.8.D	May not understand how to compose new two-dimensional shapes from other two-dimensional shapes	74	
8	15.3	2.8.D	May not be able to identify the number of cubes used to make a rectangular prism	75	
9	15.3	2.8.D	May not understand how to use different views of a rectangular prism to determine the number of cubes in it	75	

TEKS—Texas Essential Knowledge and Skills; **RtI**—Response to Intervention

Unit 4 Test (continued)

Item	Lesson	TEKS*	Common Error	Intervene with RtI* Tier 1 Lessons	Soar to Success Math
10	16.4	2.9.E	May not know the relationship between an inch and a foot	84	
11	16.4	2.9.E	May use an incorrect operation when determining the solution to a problem involving length	84	
12	16.4	2.9.E	May not know the relationship between an inch and a foot	84	
13	16.4	2.9.E	May have difficulty estimating the length of an object	84	
14	17.4	2.9.F	May not understand how to use square units to describe the area of a rectangle	85	
15	18.1	2.9.G	May not read time correctly to the nearest minute	86	51.08, 51.10
16	18.2	2.9.G	May not read time correctly to the nearest minute	87	51.11
17	18.4	2.9.G	May not read time correctly to the nearest minute	89	51.15
18	18.4	2.9.G	May not understand A.M. and P.M.	89	51.15

*TEKS—Texas Essential Knowledge and Skills; **RtI**—Response to Intervention

Unit 5 Test

Item	Lesson	TEKS*	Common Error	Intervene with RtI* Tier 1 Lessons	Soar to Success Math
1	19.3	2.10.A	May not understand how to read a bar graph	91	54.06
2	19.1	2.10.A	May misread the pictograph	90	54.05
3	19.2	2.10.B	May not read the tally chart correctly	92	54.12
4	19.6	2.10.B	May not understand how to use pictures to complete a row of a pictograph	94	
5	19.4	2.10.B	May not understand how to make a bar graph	93	54.06
6	19.4	2.10.B	May not understand how to make a bar graph	93	54.06
7	19.6	2.10.B	May not understand how to read a bar graph	94	
8	19.6	2.10.B	May misread the pictograph	94	
9	19.5	2.10.C	May not understand how to use a pictograph to solve a problem	95	
10	19.5	2.10.C	May not understand how to use a bar graph to solve an addition problem	95	
11	19.5	2.10.C	May not understand how to use a pictograph to solve a subtraction problem	95	
12	19.5	2.10.C	May not understand how to use a pictograph to solve a subtraction problem	95	

*TEKS—Texas Essential Knowledge and Skills; RtI—Response to Intervention

Unit 5 Test (continued)

Item	Lesson	TEKS*	Common Error	Intervene with RtI* Tier 1 Lessons	Soar to Success Math
13	19.5	2.10.C	May not understand how to use a bar graph to solve a subtraction problem	95	
14	19.5	2.10.C	May not understand how to use a bar graph to solve a subtraction problem	95	
15	19.7	2.10.D	May not correctly describe change that data in a bar graph shows	96	
16	19.7	2.10.D	May not know how to use a bar graph to make a prediction	96	
17	19.7	2.10.D	May not know how to use a bar graph to make a prediction	96	
18	19.7	2.10.D	May not know how to use a bar graph to make a prediction	96	

*TEKS—Texas Essential Knowledge and Skills; **RtI**—Response to Intervention

Child's Name _____ Date _____

Unit 6 Test

Item	Lesson	TEKS*	Common Error	Intervene with RtI* Tier 1 Lessons	Soar to Success Math
1	20.2	2.11.A	May not know how to correctly calculate the number of weeks it will take to save an amount of money	57	12.18
2	20.2	2.11.A	May not know how to correctly calculate how much money will be saved in a number of months	57	12.18
3	20.2	2.11.A	May not know how to correctly calculate how much money will be saved in a number of months	57	12.18
4	20.1	2.11.B	May not understand that saving involves addition and spending involves subtraction	56	3.11, 3.12
5	20.1	2.11.B	May not understand that saving involves addition and spending involves subtraction	56	3.11, 3.12
6	20.1	2.11.B	May not understand that saving involves addition and spending involves subtraction	56	3.11, 3.12
7	20.3	2.11.C	May not understand that a deposit involves addition and a withdrawal involves subtraction	32	10.34
8	20.3	2.11.C	May not understand that a deposit involves addition and a withdrawal involves subtraction	32	10.34
9	20.3	2.11.C	May not understand that a deposit involves addition	32	10.34

*TEKS—Texas Essential Knowledge and Skills; **RtI**—Response to Intervention

Unit 6 Test (continued)

Item	Lesson	TEKS*	Common Error	Intervene with RtI* Tier 1 Lessons	Soar to Success Math
10	20.4	2.11.D	May not correctly calculate the amount of money to borrow for a given purchase	38	11.23, 11.24
11	20.4	2.11.D	May not correctly calculate the amount of money to borrow for a given purchase	38	11.23, 11.24
12	20.4	2.11.D	May not correctly calculate the amount of money to borrow for a given purchase	38	11.23, 11.24
13	20.5	2.11.E	May not know how to calculate how long it will take to pay back a loan	39	11.23, 11.24
14	20.5	2.11.E	May not know how to calculate the total amount borrowed	39	11.23, 11.24
15	20.5	2.11.E	May not know how to calculate how long it will take to pay back a loan	39	11.23, 11.24
16	20.6	2.11.F	May not distinguish between a consumer and a producer	39	10.34
17	20.6	2.11.F	May not know how to calculate the cost to produce an item	39	10.34
18	20.6	2.11.F	May not know how to calculate the cost to produce an item	39	10.34

*TEKS—Texas Essential Knowledge and Skills; RtI—Response to Intervention

Correlations

Knowledge and Skills		Test/Item Numbers
2.2	**Number and operations.** The student applies mathematical process standards to understand how to represent and compare whole numbers, the relative position and magnitude of whole numbers, and relationships within the numeration system related to place value. The student is expected to:	
2.2.A	use concrete and pictorial models to compose and decompose numbers up to 1,200 in more than one way as a sum of so many thousands, hundreds, tens, and ones;	Module 1 Test: 5–8, 10, 12 Module 2 Test: 1–2 Module 3 Test: 1–3 Unit 1 Test: 1–3
2.2.B	use standard, word, and expanded forms to represent numbers up to 1,200;	Module 1 Test: 1–3 Module 2 Test: 3–4 Module 3 Test: 4–6 Unit 1 Test: 4–5 Beginning-/Middle-/End-of-Year Tests: 1
2.2.C	generate a number that is greater than or less than a given whole number up to 1,200;	Unit 1 Test: 6–7
2.2.D	use place value to compare and order whole numbers up to 1,200 using comparative language, numbers, and symbols ($>$, $<$, or $=$);	Module 2 Test: 5–8 Module 3 Test: 7–12 Unit 1 Test: 8–10 Beginning-/Middle-/End-of-Year Tests: 2, 4
2.2.E	locate the position of a given whole number on an open number line; and	Module 1 Test: 4, 11 Module 2 Test: 9–10 Beginning-/Middle-/End-of-Year Tests: 3
2.2.F	name the whole number that corresponds to a specific point on a number line.	Module 1 Test: 9 Module 2 Test: 11–12 Beginning-/Middle-/End-of-Year Tests: 5
2.3	**Number and operations.** The student applies mathematical process standards to recognize and represent fractional units and communicates how they are used to name parts of a whole. The student is expected to:	
2.3.A	partition objects into equal parts and name the parts, including halves, fourths, and eighths, using words;	Module 4 Test: 1 Unit 1 Test: 11 Beginning-/Middle-/End-of-Year Tests: 6
2.3.B	explain that the more fractional parts used to make a whole, the smaller the part; and the fewer the fractional parts, the larger the part;	Module 4 Test: 2–6 Unit 1 Test: 12–13 Beginning-/Middle-/End-of-Year Tests: 7
2.3.C	use concrete models to count fractional parts beyond one whole using words and recognize how many parts it takes to equal one whole; and	Module 4 Test: 7, 10–12 Unit 1 Test: 14–15 Beginning-/Middle-/End-of-Year Tests: 8
2.3.D	identify examples and non-examples of halves, fourths, and eighths.	Module 4 Test: 8–9 Beginning-/Middle-/End-of-Year Tests: 9

Correlations

Knowledge and Skills		Test/Item Numbers
2.4	**Number and operations.** The student applies mathematical process standards to develop and use strategies and methods for whole number computations in order to solve addition and subtraction problems with efficiency and accuracy. The student is expected to:	
2.4.A	recall basic facts to add and subtract within 20 with automaticity;	Module 5 Test: 1–8 Beginning-/Middle-/End-of-Year Tests: 10
2.4.B	add up to four two-digit numbers and subtract two-digit numbers using mental strategies and algorithms based on knowledge of place value and properties of operations;	Module 6 Test: 1–12 Module 7 Test: 1–8 Unit 1 Test: 17–18 Module 8 Test: 1–9 Module 9 Test: 1–2 Unit 2 Test: 1 Beginning-/Middle-/End-of-Year Tests: 11
2.4.C	solve one-step and multi-step word problems involving addition and subtraction within 1,000 using a variety of strategies based on place value, including algorithms; and	Module 5 Test: 9–12 Module 7 Test: 9–12 Unit 1 Test: 16 Module 8 Test: 10–12 Module 9 Test: 3–10 Module 10 Test: 1–9 Unit 2 Test: 2–5 Beginning-/Middle-/End-of-Year Tests: 12
2.4.D	generate and solve problem situations for a given mathematical number sentence involving addition and subtraction of whole numbers within 1,000.	Module 9 Test: 11–12 Module 10 Test: 10–12 Unit 2 Test: 6 Beginning-/Middle-/End-of-Year Tests: 13
2.5	**Number and operations.** The student applies mathematical process standards to determine the value of coins in order to solve monetary transactions. The student is expected to:	
2.5.A	determine the value of a collection of coins up to one dollar; and	Beginning-/Middle-/End-of-Year Tests: 14
2.5.B	use the cent symbol, dollar sign, and the decimal point to name the value of a collection of coins.	Module 11 Test: 1–12 Unit 2 Test: 7–10 Beginning-/Middle-/End-of-Year Tests: 15
2.6	**Number and operations.** The student applies mathematical process standards to connect repeated addition and subtraction to multiplication and division situations that involve equal groupings and shares. The student is expected to:	
2.6.A	model, create, and describe contextual multiplication situations in which equivalent sets of concrete objects are joined; and	Module 12 Test: 1–5 Unit 2 Test: 11–14 Beginning-/Middle-/End-of-Year Tests: 16
2.6.B	model, create, and describe contextual division situations in which a set of concrete objects is separated into equivalent sets.	Module 12 Test: 6–12 Unit 2 Test: 15–18 Beginning-/Middle-/End-of-Year Tests: 17

Correlations

Knowledge and Skills		Test/Item Numbers
2.7	**Algebraic reasoning.** The student applies mathematical process standards to identify and apply number patterns within properties of numbers and operations in order to describe relationships. The student is expected to:	
2.7.A	determine whether a number up to 40 is even or odd using pairings of objects to represent the number;	Unit 3 Test: 1 Beginning-/Middle-/End-of-Year Tests: 18
2.7.B	use an understanding of place value to determine the number that is 10 or 100 more or less than a given number up to 1,200; and	Unit 3 Test: 2–9 Beginning-/Middle-/End-of-Year Tests: 19
2.7.C	represent and solve addition and subtraction word problems where unknowns may be any one of the terms in the problem.	Unit 3 Test: 10–18 Beginning-/Middle-/End-of-Year Tests: 20
2.8	**Geometry and measurement.** The student applies mathematical process standards to analyze attributes of two-dimensional shapes and three-dimensional solids to develop generalizations about their properties. The student is expected to:	
2.8.A	create two-dimensional shapes based on given attributes, including number of sides and vertices;	Module 14 Test: 1–2 Beginning-/Middle-/End-of-Year Tests: 21
2.8.B	classify and sort three-dimensional solids, including spheres, cones, cylinders, rectangular prisms (including cubes as special rectangular prisms), and triangular prisms, based on attributes using formal geometric language;	Module 15 Test: 1–7 Unit 4 Test: 1–2 Beginning-/Middle-/End-of-Year Tests: 22
2.8.C	classify and sort polygons with 12 or fewer sides according to attributes, including identifying the number of sides and number of vertices;	Module 14 Test: 3–7 Unit 4 Test: 3–5 Beginning-/Middle-/End-of-Year Tests: 23
2.8.D	compose two-dimensional shapes and three-dimensional solids with given properties or attributes; and	Module 14 Test: 8–10 Module 15 Test: 8–12 Unit 4 Test: 6–9 Beginning-/Middle-/End-of-Year Tests: 24
2.8.E	decompose two-dimensional shapes such as cutting out a square from a rectangle, dividing a shape in half, or partitioning a rectangle into identical triangles and identify the resulting geometric parts.	Module 14 Test: 11–12 Beginning-/Middle-/End-of-Year Tests: 25
2.9	**Geometry and measurement.** The student applies mathematical process standards to select and use units to describe length, area, and time. The student is expected to:	
2.9.A	find the length of objects using concrete models for standard units of length;	Module 16 Test: 1–2 Beginning-/Middle-/End-of-Year Tests: 27
2.9.B	describe the inverse relationship between the size of the unit and the number of units needed to equal the length of an object;	Module 16 Test: 3–4 Beginning-/Middle-/End-of-Year Tests: 26

Correlations

	Knowledge and Skills	Test/Item Numbers
2.9.C	represent whole numbers as distances from any given location on a number line;	Module 17 Test: 1–4 Beginning-/Middle-/End-of-Year Tests: 28
2.9.D	determine the length of an object to the nearest marked unit using rulers, yardsticks, meter sticks, or measuring tapes;	Module 16 Test: 5–6 Module 17 Test: 5–8 Beginning-/Middle-/End-of-Year Tests: 29
2.9.E	determine a solution to a problem involving length, including estimating lengths;	Module 16 Test: 7–12 Unit 4 Test: 10–13 Beginning-/Middle-/End-of-Year Tests: 30
2.9.F	use concrete models of square units to find the area of a rectangle by covering it with no gaps or overlaps, counting to find the total number of square units, and describing the measurement using a number and the unit; and	Module 17 Test: 9–12 Unit 4 Test: 14 Beginning-/Middle-/End-of-Year Tests: 31
2.9.G	read and write time to the nearest one-minute increment using analog and digital clocks and distinguish between a.m. and p.m.	Module 18 Test: 1–12 Unit 4 Test: 15–18 Beginning-/Middle-/End-of-Year Tests: 32
2.10	**Data analysis.** The student applies mathematical process standards to organize data to make it useful for interpreting information and solving problems. The student is expected to:	
2.10.A	explain that the length of a bar in a bar graph or the number of pictures in a pictograph represents the number of data points for a given category;	Unit 5 Test: 1–2
2.10.B	organize a collection of data with up to four categories using pictographs and bar graphs with intervals of one or more;	Unit 5 Test: 3–8 Beginning-/Middle-/End-of-Year Tests: 33
2.10.C	write and solve one-step word problems involving addition or subtraction using data represented within pictographs and bar graphs with intervals of one; and	Unit 5 Test: 9–14 Beginning-/Middle-/End-of-Year Tests: 34
2.10.D	draw conclusions and make predictions from information in a graph.	Unit 5 Test: 15–18 Beginning-/Middle-/End-of-Year Tests: 35
2.11	**Personal financial literacy.** The student applies mathematical process standards to manage one's financial resources effectively for lifetime financial security. The student is expected to:	
2.11.A	calculate how money saved can accumulate into a larger amount over time;	Unit 6 Test: 1–3 Beginning-/Middle-/End-of-Year Tests: 36
2.11.B	explain that saving is an alternative to spending;	Unit 6 Test: 4–6
2.11.C	distinguish between a deposit and a withdrawal;	Unit 6 Test: 7–9 Beginning-/Middle-/End-of-Year Tests: 37
2.11.D	identify examples of borrowing and distinguish between responsible and irresponsible borrowing;	Unit 6 Test: 10–12 Beginning-/Middle-/End-of-Year Tests: 38

Correlations

Knowledge and Skills		Test/Item Numbers
2.11.E	identify examples of lending and use concepts of benefits and costs to evaluate lending decisions; and	Unit 6 Test: 13–15 Beginning-/Middle-/End-of-Year Tests: 39
2.11.F	differentiate between producers and consumers and calculate the cost to produce a simple item.	Unit 6 Test: 16–18 Beginning-/Middle-/End-of-Year Tests: 40